INTENSIVE SCHEDULING

David S. Hottenstein

INTENSIVE
SCHEDULING

Restructuring America's
Secondary Schools
Through
Time Management

CORWIN PRESS, INC.
A Sage Publications Company
Thousand Oaks, California

Copyright ©1998 by Corwin Press, Inc.

For information:

Corwin Press, Inc.
A Sage Publications Company
2455 Teller Road
Thousand Oaks, California 91320
E-mail: order@corwin.sagepub.com

SAGE Publications Ltd.
6 Bonhill Street
London EC2A 4PU
United Kingdom

SAGE Publications India Pvt. Ltd.
M-32 Market
Greater Kailash I
New Delhi 110 048 India

Printed in the United States of America

Library of Congress Cataloging-in-Publication Data

Hottenstein, David S.
    Intensive scheduling : Restructuring America's secondary schools
through time management / David S. Hottenstein.
        p.   cm.
    ISBN 0-8039-6653-9 (cloth : acid-free paper). — ISBN
0-8039-6654-7 (pbk. : acid-free paper)
        1. Schedules, School—United States.   2. Education, Secondary—
United States—Administration.   3. Time management—United States.
I. Title.
LB3032.H68   1997
373.12'42'0973—dc21   97-45259

This book is printed on acid-free paper.

98 99 00 01 02 03 10 9 8 7 6 5 4 3 2 1

Production Editor: S. Marlene Head
Editorial Assistant: Kristen L. Gibson
Typesetter: Andrea D. Swanson
Cover Designer: Marcia M. Rosenburg

Contents

Preface

Is intensive scheduling just another ill-conceived fad or a dynamic catalyst capable of transforming schools into successful organizational structures for the 21st century? Intensive scheduling, or block scheduling as it is sometimes called, has become yet another controversial educational reform initiative in America. This book centers on the difficult questions that surface about intensive scheduling and addresses burning concerns and common successes.

Intensive scheduling has been the primary focus of my professional life for the past 8 years. Two years of research and investigation followed by 6 years of implementation at the Hatboro-Horsham High School (Hatboro-Horsham is a suburban, 9 through 12 school of 1,400 students located 25 miles outside of Philadelphia), where I am Principal and Director of Secondary Education, have helped me to see how time reconfiguration can act as a powerful change agent.

During the past 4 years, I have traveled all over the United States and Canada visiting schools and speaking to more than 5,000 educators about this fascinating topic. I have also collected quantitative and qualitative data from hundreds of schools across North America. In addition, I have had contact with schools from Europe, the Middle East, and the Far East interested in learning more about intensive scheduling.

Although other books about block scheduling have done a fine job of covering this topic from a theoretical standpoint, there has been a consistent outcry for a blueprint from a practitioner's perspective.

As a result, my book will draw from personal experiences as well as those from schools across our nation. What makes this topic both intriguing and debatable is that intensive scheduling has become very diverse in concept and design. It is impossible to talk about intensive scheduling as if it is merely one concept or a single approach. In reality, the realm of block scheduling has become very sophisticated and complex, including the development of several hybrids and many variations of core themes. If viewed superficially, intensive scheduling can become misunderstood by educators and laypeople alike.

Intensive scheduling is just one important piece of the school reform puzzle that should be researched and considered when we begin to talk about restructuring schools. The main reason for considering a scheduling change at my school was uncovered by the faculty and parents as part of a schoolwide self-analysis. Parents, students, teachers, and community found that the school curriculum and organizational structure had remained basically the same for more than 30 years. It had become apparent to everyone that the traditional assembly-line schedule was standing in the way of progress at our school. We realized that although society had changed radically from 1950 through 1990, Hatboro-Horsham High School had remained academically flatlined. It was clear that the business-as-usual approach to education was no longer meeting the needs of our students as they approached the year 2000. Dr. Kyle Peck, a professor at Penn State University, says that even the best schools in America are in need of radical change. Dr. Peck points out the need for schools to remain in touch with rapidly changing societal realities, including the global economy, technology, and the information age. Staying on the cutting edge for our children will take ongoing creative thought and well-coordinated planning. More important is the need to look beyond the traditional standards, which may no longer apply, and consider the demands and challenges that our students will face now and in the future.

In the summer of 1994, the National Association of Secondary School Principals (NASSP) invited me to serve on a special commission, and that experience further shaped my educational thinking in a progressive direction. In February 1996, NASSP and the Carnegie Foundation released a publication titled *Breaking Ranks: Changing an American Institution*. It was a pleasure to work on this publication as part of a national commission that studied high school education and developed recommendations designed to help educators improve secondary schools. The commission outlined six key pillars that I believe are critical to the success of all schools. One of these pillars, of course, is time. It was clear to the commission that time and organizational structure, if organized properly, would provide a sound framework for school improvement.

Intensive Scheduling: Restructuring America's Secondary Schools Through Time Management has been written specifically for educators and laypeople interested in improving secondary schools everywhere. College professors who are preparing students to be teachers and administrators will find the book to be a practical guide. School administrators and teachers will find this book to be a credible source for professional development as they look at time as a vehicle for school restructuring. All citizens, including parents, students, and businesspeople interested in the future of education, will find that this book helps to clarify many of the controversial issues surrounding intensive scheduling.

The common denominator for success with intensive scheduling continues to be how well the concept is implemented. The key to failure lies in the inability of educational stakeholders to gain consensus on why there is a need for change. Fear, complacency, and a lack of vision are the most difficult hurdles facing school reformists. Tremendous diversity concerning politics, resources, and school/community priorities make measuring the success of intensive scheduling in any form very difficult.

Let us look ahead and preview the chapters that will follow. Chapter 1 develops a practitioner's guide on how to manage change successfully. It will take the reader through the change process step by step, from theory to practice. This chapter also helps answer the all-important question: Why change?

Chapter 2 takes a careful look inside the realm of intensive scheduling. This chapter will analyze the Hatboro-Horsham case study and also explore the national perspective. Chapter 2 clearly defines what this initiative is and how diverse it has become. Why has this school reform initiative, like many others before it, become controversial? Why is the word "fad" being connected to the logical idea of time reconfiguration? This chapter will examine a variety of intensive scheduling models from both a mechanical and instructional viewpoint.

Chapter 3 explains how to train teachers to teach in a longer block of time. It will cover the areas of instructional strategies, classroom

management, curriculum pacing, and assessment. This chapter out-
lines the parameters and guidelines needed for successful teaching
and carefully analyzes the benefits of intensive scheduling.

Chapter 4 takes the professional development piece and applies
it inside the intensive scheduling classroom. This chapter will examine the implementation of instructional strategies, curriculum coverage, and assessment issues. Chapter 4 will address problem areas and
pitfalls of teaching in a longer block of time and the impact that
different block schedules have on each subject area.

Chapter 5 looks at how intensive scheduling will positively affect
curriculum development and technology utilization. The positive
relationships between intensive scheduling, curriculum, and technology are carefully analyzed.

Chapter 6 analyzes the critical phase of program evaluation. One
of my greatest fears as I look at intensive scheduling is the lack of
proper and thorough evaluation. Both internal and external models
will be studied from a quantitative and qualitative perspective.

The epilogue gives me an opportunity to share my vision for
secondary schools of the future. From the perspective of time and
organization, and using *Breaking Ranks* as a guide, I will explain which
components must be present if schools are going to be successful in
meeting the needs of their students.

After reading this book, I hope you will have a better understanding about intensive scheduling, how it works, and why it is
better than traditional scheduling. Intensive scheduling is not, however, a magic wand, nor is it the answer to all of our educational
problems. Instead, flexible scheduling is a viable school reform initiative that all schools should at least research and consider as they try
to improve their academic programs.

Acknowledgments

My entire life, I have been surrounded by a wonderful family and
many loyal friends. These individuals have guided and supported my
personal and professional pursuits enthusiastically. My wife, Nancy,
and my sons, Brian and Andrew, have been my greatest inspiration.
My parents, brother, and sister have provided me with a sound
personal foundation. I am indebted also to my bosses, Dr. Clifford

Hendrickson, and presently, Dr. Gerald Strock, who have both guided me as a professional along the way. Finally, special thanks to Millie Walker and Connie Malatesta for helping me make this book a reality.

There have also been dozens of other people who have helped me gather information, shared experiences, and worked with me in developing my knowledge base over the past 8 years. In addition to those I have already mentioned, I would like to acknowledge the following for their help and dedication.

The Hatboro-Horsham School Board

The Hatboro-Horsham faculty, parents, and students

Mr. Samuel James Worthington

The National Commission on *Breaking Ranks*

Dr. Timothy J. Dyer, NASSP

Dr. John A. Lammel, NASSP

Dr. Thomas Koerner, NASSP

Ms. Lenor Hersey, NASSP

Mr. James Sullivan

Dr. John Cornelius

Ms. Christine Coleman

The Improvement of Instruction Committee

Dr. E. Donald Brown

Dr. Leroy Huff

Mr. Chuck Paradisio

Dr. Preston Feden

Dr. Robert Vogel

Father Paul Kennedy

Dr. Kit Marshall

Dr. Thomas Short

Ms. Susan Goldsmith

Dr. Dale Spaulding

Dr. Dorothy Kueny

Mrs. Judy Ehlenberger

About the Author

David S. Hottenstein graduated from the University of Delaware in 1971 and received his Principal's certificate from Villanova University. He was Principal of Keith Valley Middle School from 1978 to 1980 and has been Principal of the Hatboro-Horsham High School since 1981. Mr. Hottenstein began to restructure the high school in 1989, and this led to a very successful program referred to as intensive scheduling (4 × 4 + 1 semester scheduling). His efforts at his own school and in working with educators across the nation have gained him considerable attention and acclaim. He was the 1994 Pennsylvania Principal of the Year, was one of seven principals nationwide named to the Carnegie Foundation/NASSP National Commission on High School Restructuring (see *Breaking Ranks*), received the Delaware Valley ASCD "Excellence in Education Award" in 1995, and most recently, received the 1996 Milken Family Foundation National Educators Award. Mr. Hottenstein's leadership helped the Hatboro-Horsham High School become a nationally recognized Blue Ribbon School in 1996 and also one of *Redbook* magazine's "Top 150 America's Best Schools" in the "overall excellence" category. He also does consulting to individual schools or organizations sponsoring workshops. Keynotes, half-day, full-day, or multiple-day programs are available on a variety of restructuring topics, including alternative scheduling.

1

Change: Why It's Necessary and How to Manage It

A successful change process is at least as important as any positive school reform initiative, such as intensive scheduling. No matter how sound any restructuring idea may be, the ability to move a school organization successfully through the tricky gauntlet of change remains the greatest challenge for educators at all levels. Developing a well-coordinated plan that will take a school community from theory to practice is critical to continuous school improvement. I have found that once schools are able to navigate a change process and reach a successful conclusion, other positive changes often follow.

We have learned from the study of human psychology that human beings are creatures of habit and, generally speaking, are resistant to change. Although many educators are open to change, I have found some to be fearful and others to be complacent, continually holding on to the status quo at all costs. Consistent with other institutions, there are always a recalcitrant few in education who are just purely lazy and disinterested in any ideas that may represent more work or a different approach. Another group of people both inside and outside of the profession are against any reform initiative coming from within the educational institution. In many cases, educators have created these negative groups of extremists by repeatedly failing with the process of change. The public has become cynical about the inability of educators to handle effectively the difficult business of change. Some reform ideas have been received poorly, others have been implemented improperly, and, even worse, few have been measured adequately. These problems—coupled with leadership that is either unable or unwilling to take risks, gain consensus, or lead assertively—have soured the public's confidence in some pockets of American education.

My father, a lifelong educator, once explained, "School reformists have the life expectancy of a fruit fly." His observation from 35 years in education accurately points out the dangers and pitfalls that await even the best educational leaders. I also believe what Dr. Kyle Peck, a professor from Penn State University, believes—that even the best of America's schools are in need of radical change. Dr. Peck points out that the one constant in life is change, and we must continue to change in order to improve. Ongoing change is also needed to keep pace with a fast-moving, ever-changing society. At a very basic level, our schools align with society and prepare young people for a career, family living, and citizenship. What students need to know and be able to do today differs greatly from past decades. In addition, what students will need to know and accomplish as they enter the 21st century continues to change rapidly.

So where do we start, and how do we build a successful blueprint so that positive changes are possible? How do you get your school from theory to practice?

Do a Schoolwide Self-Analysis

Gain consensus on what is working and what needs to improve. You must answer the question: Why change? Your self-analysis can help you get the answer and may dovetail with a long-range planning process for a regional self-evaluation. Many schools develop their own site-based analysis. Every aspect of the school culture should be probed and critiqued, and all of the key stakeholders must be involved in this process. Making up questions, evaluating the data, developing trends, and making recommendations for the future should be shared by administrators, school board, parents, students, teachers, and community alike. This process should include a review of your school's past. Where have you been? Have positive changes been made over the years? Have you stayed in touch with societal changes and demands, or are you using 1960 standards to measure school success in 1997? How different is your academic program now from what it was in 1967, 1977, and 1987? Look at all aspects of your school program, including scheduling, facilities, environment, discipline, curriculum, instruction, technology, and organizational structure.

What drives your school's academic program? Typically, higher education admission standards, classes for the academically talented, outdated textbooks, assembly-line scheduling, traditional methodology, and special needs classes for lower functioning students drive high schools across our country. In addition, despite student-friendly rhetoric, many schools make decisions based on what is good for the adults in the organization and not necessarily what is good for the students. Many schools talk about shared decision making, but in reality, most decisions come from the top down. Some administrators believe that this approach is necessary because many teachers have been resistant to change in the past, which has led to several failures. Parents have either watched these failures from the sidelines or felt the negative results firsthand, which has made them wary of educational reform in general. All of this creates a vicious cycle that makes managing any change very difficult.

Once the self-analysis is complete, use the information collected to start the process and to support your findings with credible outside sources. *Breaking Ranks: Changing an American Institution* (National Association of Secondary School Principals, 1996) is a good example of a credible source that could help you gain consensus on key issues. There are dozens of experts, reports, books, and periodicals that can provide experiences and supportive data that will guide you through the process of change. More important, use your own experiences, and above all else, use common sense! The facts are clear! In 1930, 85% of our workers were involved in agriculture, whereas in 1997, less than 3% work in that industry. Since 1940, our population has exploded, space travel is commonplace, major organ transplants are routine, test-tube babies are born daily, satellites control world communication, plastic money replaces paper currency, computers and robots dominate the global economy, and 73% of items found on supermarket shelves today did not exist 50 years ago. Society has changed radically, whereas our schools have remained status quo even though our students will live and work in this ever-changing new world.

Use the outside data you collect and your site-based self-analysis to help answer the question, "Why change?" Get the key stakeholders talking about the need for change, and decide on the first step. Obviously, I believe that time and organization are the logical places to start the restructuring process.

Develop a Plan and Timeline

Assuming that time is your focus and all of the key stakeholders were involved in the self-analysis, decide on where you are headed and what you hope to accomplish. Establish clear-cut expectations, and define what success means to your school. My definition for success, no matter what the change initiative, includes the following components:

1. Improving the school environment
   a. Discipline
   b. Attitude
   c. Facility
   d. Resources
2. Improving instruction inside the classroom
3. Improving student achievement results

Most schools that meet with this definition of success start the change process with a committee of 15 to 20 key people representing all of the stakeholders. This group, which might be called the site-based council or the advisory committee, must accomplish certain goals:

1. Develop a school mission statement. What are the purposes of your school?
2. Based on the self-analysis, select your key change (time and organization).
3. Develop a plan and timeline, including subcommittees for specific study in key areas (evaluation, professional development, parent-student orientation, and scheduling mechanics).

4. Formulate a long-range goal or vision (more efficient and effective use of time for instruction that will eventually yield better academic results).

5. Establish short-term expectations and objectives (better teaching and learning environment, more interactive instruction, and better use of technology).

6. Measure everything you do from both a quantitative and a qualitative perspective (take at least 1 year of baseline data compared to 2 years or more of the key change).

Get From Theory (Key Change) to Practice (Implementation) Successfully

My experience has shown clearly that the subcommittee structure is the key at this point in the process. Possible subcommittees directly relating to scheduling could look like this:

1. Evaluation and measurement
2. Professional development
3. Parent-student orientation
4. Scheduling mechanics

Once again, keep all of the key stakeholders involved, and make sure they are represented on each committee that needs its own plan and timeline after it receives its charge from the administration or site-based council. All subcommittees should try to stay on a similar time schedule for proper coordination. Monthly or quarterly reports are suggested. These reports should be communicated to the parents, community, students, school board, and staff in writing and verbally at public meetings. There should be time for discussion and questions after important information has been disseminated. Concerns will typically arise from recalcitrant teachers, parents of academically talented students, extremists, high school seniors, and politically motivated groups. Address these groups and their concerns head on! Include these individuals in the process—meet one-on-one, and send them out to see the successful reform initiative you are considering at other locations. Answer their questions, and give them credible information. Most important, dismantle the negative information they may provide in an intelligent, surgical manner by presenting both empirical data and experience that counters their attacks.

Each one of these areas will be addressed in greater detail in future chapters. In brief, however, the charge for each committee must be specific:

1. *Evaluation and measurement.* Develop a qualitative and quantitative baseline study of at least 1 year but hopefully 2 years. Compare this data against at least 2 years of your new initiative. This committee should develop a list of criteria, as well as questions for an anonymous qualitative survey that will be taken anonymously by parents, students, and teachers each year.

2. *Professional development.* This subcommittee should be site based and include inside training, possibly with the help of outside experts or facilitators. Videotapes, conference calling, and visitations in the field are imperative. Start this process with a survey of students and staff to find out how teachers instruct now. What are the strengths and weaknesses of your professional staff presently? Ask questions about homework, assessment, and curriculum delivery. Address the issue of passive versus interactive instruction, and which is better for learning. Develop teaching competencies for your professional staff that are tied into both curriculum and skills. This committee must recognize that the roles of both teacher and student will most likely change inside the classroom no matter what reform initiative is selected.

3. *Parent-student orientation.* Subcommittees 2 and 3 are closely related and, in some instances, may even interact together. Follow a similar process (like Subcommittee 2) but from a different viewpoint. Answer their questions, and get them involved in visitations. Get them to think about the classroom experience, especially the learning process. Do not expect students and parents to jump on the reform bandwagon just because you say it is better. Be prepared to address the parents of academically talented students. They usually struggle with the thought of change because for them, the present system is not broken. The key is to get them involved and help them to realize that their students will succeed in any system but will flourish in a more positive and flexible academic environment. Your goal should be to give them information and answer their questions in the hope of keeping their minds open about the new idea.

4. *Scheduling mechanics.* This subcommittee should be made up primarily of school board members, educators, and students, but other representatives are welcome. Establish a list of existing realities, and identify key problem areas. Existing realities might include lunches, busing, state mandates, union contracts, and sacred courses or curriculum areas. Develop your conversion rate by identifying the characteristics of your present schedule and what will happen to the school day when you convert to the new time configuration. Each organizational component of your school should be given the opportunity to develop a wish list of ways that they can improve instruction and results if time is organized a certain way. Remember, some of the best decisions are made as close to the classroom as possible.

Move on to the Next Key Change!

Remember, change is a constant and is needed if your school is to improve on an ongoing basis. Change is a process, *not* an event. If you hope to stay in touch with the complex, ever-changing, fast-moving society we live in, change is inevitable. Do not fight the need for change; instead, strive to deal with it effectively. Schools that can handle the change process effectively have the ability to take even a mediocre idea and be successful. Conversely, schools that are in conflict can fail no matter how strong the reform initiative may be.

In Conclusion

I remember the early days of change at Hatboro-Horsham. Keep in mind that in 1989, when we started the process, Hatboro-Horsham was considered a good school using traditional standards. It was a tumultuous and difficult period. My urge was to rationalize and revert to the status quo. Staying the course was safe and, after all, we were doing just fine using traditional standards. But my conscience would not allow me to look the other way. I knew that our school needed to restructure in an effort to better meet the needs of the students. During the initial restructuring steps, my staff broke down into three groups. One third was excited, one third was clipping grenades to its belts, and one third was somewhere in the middle, refusing to commit in any direction. (Sound familiar?) This type of breakdown is very typical and presents a formidable challenge. The process I have outlined in this chapter has been used by hundreds of schools across America and has been very successful. Most schools find that a year or two provides enough time to do the job well, but in reality, each educational organization must tailor the process and timeline to meet its own needs. Most important, the key stakeholders need to build the new idea and commit to it.

So why and how do schools fail at the process of change?

1. They try to do too much at one time—the school reform platter gets cluttered. Teachers and administrators lose focus. Seldom, if ever, does any one initiative get completed properly.

2. They rush the process—a school decides in April to put a new schedule in place the following September. There is no involvement and no time for planning or preparation.

3. Top-down decisions are made—administrators make a decision and force it down the stakeholders' throats—good luck!

4. The key stakeholders are not all involved—administrators and/or staff work in isolation on a new program or idea, then spring the change on the other stakeholders. Involve everyone from the beginning.

5. Resources are lacking—you do not need "state-of-the-art" resources, but the cupboard should not be depleted, either. Reasonable supplies and equipment need to be provided.

6. Facilities are inadequate—schools have an obligation to maintain a safe and clean learning environment. You do not, however, need a palace! Take pride in your facility and grounds.

7. There is a lack of trust among the key stakeholders—establish fair ground rules and an opportunity for open communication on a daily basis. Be upfront and honest at all times.

8. Counterproductive politics exist—there is *no* place for politics in education. Politics should *stop* at the schoolhouse door! (Who said that?)

9. Union strife exists—when unions and school systems cannot agree, children suffer. The union process must be kept in the proper perspective. School systems must be fair to their employees! Whenever a union strike takes place, everybody inside the educational equation loses!

10. There is a lack of professional development—without this essential component, very little, if any, change will take place inside the classroom.

11. There is a lack of evaluation and measurement—if school reform is not measured, accountability is lacking. The change process needs feedback in order to make adjustments and improvements.

12. There is not enough staff to do the job well—competent and dedicated staff members are still our most valuable resource.

More times than not, we can find the reasons that schools fail with change on this list. My experience has shown clearly that most school reform ideas will work well if they are built and implemented properly. However, even the best ideas are doomed to failure if educators do not learn to manage the process of change effectively.

Let's now look forward more specifically to the prospect of time and organization as the first steps in the restructuring process. What does intensive scheduling look like? Why is intensive scheduling better? How do you build intensive scheduling properly? What are the different options to consider in an effort to tailor this idea to meet the needs of each individual school? Chapter 2 will answer all of these questions.

2

Restructuring Through Time Management

Your school clearly sees a need for change in at least one area. The key stakeholders have developed a well-coordinated plan to ensure a step-by-step process that will take the key change from theory to practice successfully. Where do you start, and what should the first step include?

First, you must ascertain which educational components you control and identify the existing realities that, under any circumstances, will be difficult to change. The key stakeholders at most schools have at least some input into five basic areas. Let's examine each area carefully as we begin to consider where to begin the restructuring process.

1. *Curriculum/Skill Development.* Typically, teachers are empowered to establish guidelines and core concepts in each area of study. Textbooks, software, activities, instructional strategies, pacing, and assessment are usually developed and managed by the professional staff. Although governing bodies often influence this process and give their approval, teachers usually are asked to build the academic program and deliver the curriculum so that students understand the concepts and can apply them. State mandates and local forces often

give strong directions on how a curriculum should be structured and implemented. In addition, textbook companies, software manufacturers, and the mass media have easy access and tremendous influence on the flow of information into schools. Remember that your curriculum should include a balance between skill development and core concepts.

2. *Instructional Strategies.* How well teachers plan for the classroom and deliver the instructional package is critical to student learning. The interaction between teacher and students inside the classroom is where the rubber meets the road. The amount of time a teacher spends on a key concept and which teaching styles are used will either stimulate a student's brain or possibly turn it off totally. Learning styles and teaching styles must accommodate each other at every turn. How students learn must drive appropriate decisions about methodology. The seven multiple intelligences and brain functions must be understood by every teacher and must be considered when planning the daily classroom experience. Well-organized activities where methods shift two, three, or four times per unit of learning is critical. Emphasis must be placed on interactive approaches where students are expected to become engaged in their own learning. Teachers who continue to instruct in ways that make them comfortable on topics they enjoy need to change or be assertively redirected by their superiors. The use of graphic organizers and a variety of assessments properly aligned with the curriculum are also imperative if we hope to improve classroom instruction. Most important is that we need to remember to personalize the academic program, develop student-centered classrooms, and emphasize learning above all else. Remember, coverage alone without learning is counterproductive.

3. *Grouping.* The best way to organize and structure classes for instruction has been debated for years by people inside and outside of education. The argument over heterogeneous versus homogeneous grouping has been analyzed for decades. Typically, middle schools tend to dabble with heterogeneous grouping but slide toward homogeneous organization in reading and math, especially for the academically talented student. Most high schools, however, have stayed enamored of homogeneous grouping, which includes special groups for the gifted and challenged. This approach often leaves a vast wasteland of students floundering in the middle. Although heterogeneous

grouping is most frequently found in elective subjects, it is seldom present for the "core" curriculum. I never understood how schools could provide personalized programs for bright students and those with deficiencies, yet seemingly assume that all of the remaining students would somehow be all right. How well we teach, rather than grouping, will have the greatest impact on student achievement.

4. *Time and Organization. Breaking Ranks: Changing an American Institution* made the following statement: "The manner in which a high school organizes itself and the ways in which it uses time create a framework that affects almost everything about teaching and learning in the school" (NASSP, 1996, p. 44). Flexible time use is a powerful catalyst that helps to place teachers and students into better teaching and learning environments. Longer blocks of time provide more flexibility for different instructional strategies that will accommodate a variety of learning styles. Time serves as the framework and foundation for the curriculum delivery system within a school. It is a popular starting point for the school improvement process because time surrounds and affects each person's behavior and every aspect of educational life. How efficiently we organize our time and how effectively we use it greatly influences the quality of our daily lives. For two decades, businesses, organizations, and institutions have used time management as a springboard for successful restructuring to improve productivity and quality control.

Why does education continue to hold on to the assembly-line time schedule when clearly there are more efficient alternatives? Comfort, complacency, and fear of the unknown are probable answers that don't hold up when we consider the tremendous need for change. The traditional mode of scheduling often dictates passive teaching and passive learning. Coverage drives methodology and assessment, leaving little time for skill integration or application of core concepts. If time is reconfigured and tailored to meet the needs of students and teachers alike, it can improve instruction drastically. Conversely, the status quo will continue to give us what we have always had. National reports, feedback from the global economy, and university studies repeatedly show that business as usual will not give students the knowledge base they need or the skills they must have to meet modern societal challenges.

5. *Technology.* Although the computer age is upon us and has become commonplace in our daily lives, there is a great deal of

diversity between school systems across the country concerning the availability of technology and how it affects the educational program. Technology, like time and grouping, is a catalyst rather than a magic wand designed to transform instruction and ensure improved student achievement. School systems that throw millions of dollars of technology at teachers without a well-coordinated plan, infrastructure, or training will not realize the potential benefits of their investment. Technology delivers its greatest punch when teachers become proficient and comfortable at integrating these interactive tools into the classroom smoothly and naturally. Technology in our schools should be as natural as picking up a fork at dinner or a toothbrush each morning. Once teachers have mastered technology competencies, they will carry the information into the classroom for students to use. I like to break technology into four parts as follows:

   a. Hardware-critical mass
   b. Infrastructure and wiring—cable, networks, and Internet access
   c. Software-access information and organize data
   d. Humanware-trained teachers using technology as an interactive creative tool inside the classroom

Remember, every school needs to view the use of technology as a standard tool that all students need. It is every bit as necessary as the textbook in our traditional system of education. Technology in isolation is not, however, the answer to school improvement. It needs to be an integral part of a well-organized package that starts with smart time management. Schools need to provide flexible time configurations that will open the door for frequent technology usage, skill integration, and curriculum applications.

   The five basic areas are critical cogs in the educational wheel in every school. Selecting a starting point from these may seem difficult at first. You must analyze the data from your self-analysis for direction and develop a priority list of concerns. Most important, you want your first key change to have the greatest sweeping impact possible. Avoid tunnel vision—instead look at the big picture! Which of the five areas will reach the farthest and act as a catalyst that will touch many parts of the school infrastructure and ensure success? Obviously, I believe time and organization influence everything else that happens inside a school.

Assuming that time is your starting point, what are the options? No matter how you reconfigure your time schedule, the primary goal should be to accomplish the following:

1. Organize time more efficiently.
2. Use time more effectively for instruction.
3. Balance the curriculum delivery system between the essential learnings (what students need to know) and the essential skills (communication, problem solving, critical thinking, technology, and life skills).

These three basic ideas make a great deal of common sense and defy the notion that alternative scheduling is just another ill-conceived fad. Skeptics need to look beyond the educational landscape to understand the power of effective time management. Finally, the assembly-line organizational model gradually has become an endangered species that is seldom used by anyone in the 1990s except schools.

National Perspective

One of my greatest concerns deals with the notion that critics of block scheduling tend to use general labels that are misleading. Some naysayers would have you believe that all block schedules are created equal. Nothing could be further from the truth. Block scheduling is both complex and diverse in concept and design. Depending on their design, different block schedules will yield a variety of benefits, and possibly some drawbacks, too.

It is extremely important to seek the facts about alternative scheduling from credible sources. A credible source may be defined as someone who has at least 2 years of practical experience and the empirical data to support his or her work in the field. On the Internet and in articles, I have uncovered hundreds of cases where uninformed people with little or no experience have been quoted as experts on this topic. One of the greatest examples of this type of situation came from an excellent study out of the University of British Columbia about math and science achievement in schools implementing block scheduling. Naysayers conveniently took parts of the study out of context and published misleading reports on the Internet that made the information look credible. When I looked beyond the confusion, reality set in rapidly. First, the educational system practiced in British Columbia is culturally quite different from most American approaches. Second, block scheduling was primarily a top-down decision that came on the heels of union strife over salaries and jobs. There was little or no training for teachers during the transition. Finally, the block schedule implemented was the quarterly block, which offers students two classes per day for 9 weeks and switches to two new courses every quarter. This form of block scheduling is seldom found in America. Despite the facts, proponents of block scheduling had to fight the inaccuracies created by this manipulative portrayal.

In yet another instance, a high school math teacher was quoted in the *NCTM Bulletin* stating all of the reasons that intensive scheduling is wrong for math instruction. When I investigated the situation, I found that he had never taught 1 minute in an intensive schedule, and his background was extremely limited on the topic.

What do credible sources say about the intensive scheduling initiative from a national perspective?

1. The research data varies on scheduling usage. Depending on which study you read, 30% to 50% of America's high schools have changed to some type of block schedule. About 10% to 20% of middle schools and junior high schools have also changed.

2. Another 20% to 30% are planning to move soon or are studying the idea.

3. The three most popular scheduling models in America are
   a. 4 × 4 semester
   b. Alternating-day block 8
   c. Trimester (6 and 9 block)

   Interestingly, each schedule has a significant following across the nation and may yield different results depending on how it is implemented. In some cases, certain geographical regions of the county have latched on to one particular schedule for reasons that meet the needs of schools in that area.

4. Each one of the core scheduling models can be modified into multiple variations called "hybrids."

5. Because instruction and results will be greatly intensified and, in most cases, improved, intensive scheduling is one of many labels connected with the initiative.

6. Most researchers are reporting an 80% or better success rate for intensive scheduling when implemented properly. Results from both the quantitative and qualitative side clearly show that schools prefer some form of block scheduling over the traditional assembly-line approach.

7. Those schools that represent the 20% or less that fail usually can find the reasons for their downfall on the list found at the conclusion of Chapter 1. Typically, poor implementation, not block scheduling, dooms the success rate.

Let's take a look at the most commonly used scheduling models that are part of the intensive scheduling approach.

4 × 4 Semester

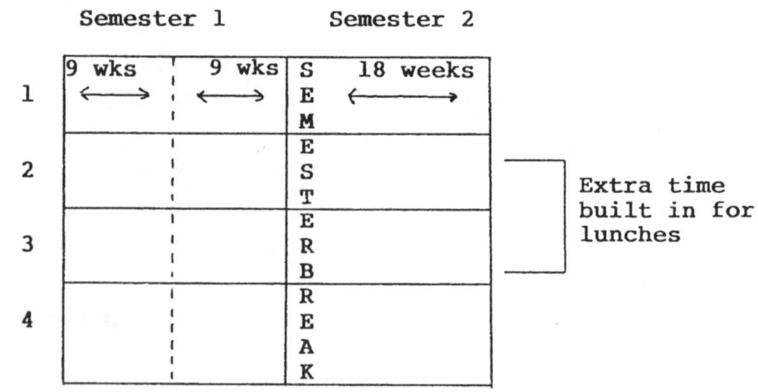

Figure 2.1. 4 × 4 Semester Schedule

The 4 × 4 semester schedule (Figure 2.1) provides students with the ability to take at least seven academic classes per year. Usually, one block is set aside for health, physical education, or other required courses depending on state and local mandates. Nine-week block classes represent one-half credit opportunities, and 18-week blocks are one-credit courses. Teachers typically have no more than three classes per semester (six for the year) and 90 students maximum at a time. Students usually have no more than three rigorous academic classes per semester. Study halls are often eliminated. Advanced placement courses may be taught first or second semester, for three quarters, or for the entire year. Some schools provide additional seminar classes or 27-week courses that supplement advanced placement instruction. Teachers normally have one full block of prep time, although some schools choose to split a block, half for preparation and half for a duty. In most cases, blocks usually range in length from a low of 75 minutes to a high of 120 minutes. Many schools allow students to accelerate (take sequential courses in succession) and remediate because greater academic capacity is often available. Successful music programs with multiple performing groups can be accommodated by implementing scheduling hybrids, including enhancement blocks, or developing rotations throughout the school year during one particular block.

In the 4 × 4 + 1 semester schedule (Figure 2.2), everything is the same as in the pure 4 × 4 semester schedule with the exception of the enhancement block, which can be structured in different ways and used for different purposes. These are local decisions. The enhancement period is often created by reorganizing existing time. For example, at Hatboro-Horsham, we virtually eliminated large chunks of time provided for teachers before and after school. We had been trying to use this time for planning, remediation, performing arts, cocurricular activities, and disciplinary issues, but we felt that this time in its traditional form was ineffective. By taking these teacher buffer times, coupled with shorter lunch periods and fewer passing times, we were able to create our enhancement period.

In some cases, students are assigned to study halls supervised by duty aides for accountability purposes, and from there, they filter into whatever opportunities the enhancement period provides. In other cases, enhancement time is unstructured particularly when an open campus environment is present. Other schools assign students to specific teachers for the purpose of advisement or mentoring. Using the enhancement period for daily performing arts practices and instruction is also an option. Advanced placement seminar classes can be held at this time. Teachers may have structured responsibilities or simply be available for students for a variety of purposes. Teachers may also plan or meet in committees or as departments at this time.

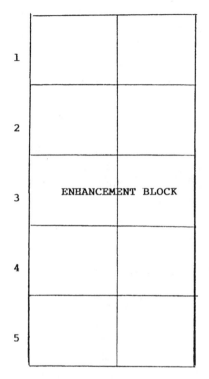

Figure 2.2. 4 × 4 + 1 Semester Schedule

The enhancement period may also be part of a 1- or 2-day-per-week altered schedule and may not occur on a daily basis. Clearly, enhancement periods provide flexible time to supplement the core schedule to better meet the needs of students and staff. These blocks may appear at the beginning, middle, or end of each day. The middle block is very popular because it accommodates lunch and gives you a captive audience at a natural break time.

Once again, in the 3 × 3 + 2 semester schedule (Figure 2.3), the basic 4 × 4 concept applies. The unique characteristic of this hybrid is the ability to split any block into two periods that run all year long for whatever purposes you desire. Music, foreign language, and math are popular considerations. Staffing and the need to couple two classes together can create logistical headaches. Enhancement periods are also difficult to schedule but not impossible. This schedule is particularly

	Semester 1		Semester 2	
1	9 wk	9 wk	18 weeks	90 min.
2				90 min.
3				90 min.
4A				45 min.*
4B				45 min.*

Figure 2.3. 3 × 3 + 2 Semester Schedule

*These periods called skinnies run all year long. This block could fall anywhere (1 through 4) within a student's schedule.

popular with middle schools and junior high schools because they can use the split period to accommodate electives and team planning periods. Middle schools often will create year-long language arts blocks and math blocks. Science and social studies are usually split into semester courses. Middle school schedules sometimes have homeroom periods at the start and end of the school day and also may create time for advisement or enhancement periods on a daily or weekly basis.

Possible Advantages of the 4 × 4 Concept

1. There is more focus and less diversion for students and teachers.
2. Teachers have fewer students per term or semester.
3. Students balance only three or four courses at a time each semester.
4. There is less stress.
5. Teachers have fewer preps (three per term).
6. There is more uninterrupted time on tasks in the classroom.
7. This approach creates instructional flexibility—shifting of methods and greater interactivity.

8. This approach integrates technology.

9. There is more time for application of concepts (hands-on activities).

10. There is more time for quality assessments.

11. There is more time for guided practice (working with students in small groups or individually).

12. This approach resembles a college model (which is important for college-bound students).

13. Teachers cannot lecture as much and must be better prepared.

14. Teachers and students get to know each other better.

15. There is usually greater student capacity for academics (more electives).

16. There is a midyear refreshment.

Possible Disadvantages of the 4 × 4 Concept

1. Sequential gaps may create a retention problem for some students (although the experience and data from the field do not support this notion).

2. Longer blocks, if not managed properly by teachers, may be boring and could create discipline problems.

3. Transferring in or out of a block schedule may create logistical problems.

4. Advanced placement classes, if not carefully scheduled or supplemented, may result in lower test scores.

5. Longer study halls for students not interested in academic pursuits are difficult to handle.

6. Scheduling performing music groups may be difficult logistically depending on which hybrid you select.

Alternating-Day Block 8

A popular variation of the intensive 4 × 4 approach is Alternating-Day Block 8 scheduling (Figure 2.4). All of the models previously shown are applicable. The major difference lies in how the school year is configured. The 4 × 4 schedule divides the year into two terms or semesters. Each semester focuses on three or four different courses, and teachers deal with approximately 60 to 90 students per term. The alternating-day approach rotates a different schedule every other day. On Day 1, for example, a

	MONDAY	TUESDAY	WEDNESDAY	THURSDAY	FRIDAY	
1						1
	D	D	D	D		2
	A	A	A	A	D	
2	Y	Y	Y	Y	A	3
					Y	4
3	1	2	1	2	3	5
						6
4						7
						8
					ENHANCEMENT	9

Figure 2.4. Alternating-Day Block 8 Schedule

student will have three or four classes; Day 2, he or she will have the same number of different classes (three or four). Students will juggle seven or eight different teachers and courses on a rotation that evolves throughout the entire school year. Teachers still have five or six classes to prepare for and teach. The student-to-teacher ratio usually remains somewhere between 140-to-1 to 180-to-1 on the average, all year long. Some schools do the Day 1/Day 2 approach, whereas others may insert a special schedule at planned intervals (weekly, biweekly, or monthly) for a variety of purposes, such as field trips, assemblies, remediation, or cocurricular activities. One common example is represented in Figure 2.4. In this concept, Day 3 students would see all of their classes for shorter periods and possibly have an enhancement block where educational needs may be supplemented.

Keep in mind that although intensive 4 × 4 semester scheduling and the alternating-day block 8 are both block schedules, they are very different in concept and design.

Possible Advantages of Alternating-Day Block 8 Concept

1. The fear of retention loss and sequential gaps dissipates.
2. Music program needs are easier to meet and schedule.
3. Math and foreign language teachers tend to be less afraid of the impact on instruction and results.
4. The longer block provides all of the same instructional and academic benefits listed under the 4 × 4 semester schedule.
5. Enhancement blocks are still possible.
6. Typically, greater student academic capacity is realized.

Possible Disadvantages of Alternating-Day Block 8 Concept

1. Students still juggle six to eight teachers every other day all year long.
2. Teachers still manage 140 to 180 students every other day all year long. This includes preparation, motivation, evaluation, and delivery of both the curriculum and skills.
3. There is no mid-year refreshment.
4. Alternating classes and the time schedule every other day may be more, not less, stressful.
5. Academic focus and continuity may be disrupted by alternating days for teachers and students.

Trimester Block

Another interesting variation of the intensive scheduling theme is trimester block scheduling. Assuming a 180-day school year, each trimester would be 60 days. There are two common forms of trimester scheduling (shown in Figures 2.5 and 2. 6).

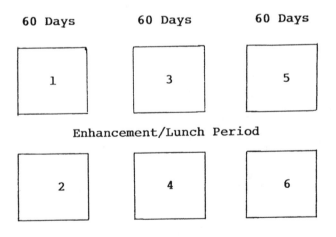

Figure 2.5. Six-Block Trimester Schedule

The six-block trimester schedule (Figure 2.5) offers one morning (a.m.) block and one afternoon (p.m.) block. Blocks may also be split to meet local program needs and for additional flexibility.

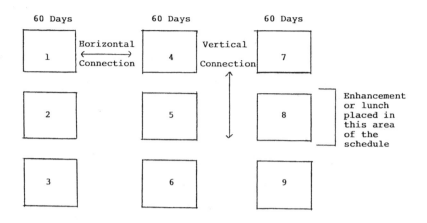

Figure 2.6. Nine-Block Trimester Schedule

The most intriguing characteristic about the nine-block trimester schedule (Figure 2.6) is flexibility. Instead of splitting blocks, which is sometimes done with the six-block schedule, the nine-block schedule provides the opportunity for connecting blocks horizontally or vertically. Horizontal connections provide longer stretches of instruction (possibly 120 days) for the purpose of advanced placement courses or international baccalaureate programs. Vertical connections give students and teachers more intensive, uninterrupted time each day on tasks. Both approaches present interesting and creative program and instructional opportunities.

Possible Advantages of Trimester Block Scheduling Concept

1. The instructional benefits of a longer block remain consistent with our other scheduling formats.
2. Tremendous flexibility and creative possibilities exist for scheduling (connecting, splitting, enhancement, seminars, etc.).
3. This approach provides greater potential academic capacity.
4. Greater elective, remediation, and enrichment opportunities exist.
5. This approach works extremely well if year-long schooling is present or with extended school years.

Possible Disadvantages of Trimester Block Scheduling Concept

1. Sequential gaps could be greater, which creates fear of retention loss.
2. It may be more expensive (room needs, staffing, etc.).
3. Logistically, it can be difficult to schedule and staff.
4. In some configurations, blocks may be too long for some teachers and students to handle on a daily basis.

Now that we understand what the different intensive schedules look like, let's consider logistics and mechanics. The best way to design a new, improved time schedule starts by analyzing your existing realities:

How many periods do you have now?

How long are they?

Do you have study halls?

How many lunches do you need?

What are your graduation requirements?

How do electives fit in?

How many classes do your teachers instruct?

How many classes do students take presently?

Are you tight on classroom space?

Do you have a lot of singletons?

Do you share staff?

What are your busing restrictions?

What does the teacher contract look like?

What are the health and physical education requirements?

What does your music program look like?

How many advanced placement courses do you offer?

How many courses or curriculum areas are "sacred cows"?

Do you want to provide remediation and enrichment opportunities?

Will you allow students to accelerate (take sequential courses in succession, one semester after the other) in subject areas such as math and foreign language?

When you reorganize the traditional schedule into an intensive schedule, have you found new time that may be used more effectively to help you meet educational goals or solve existing problems (enhancement periods, seminar classes, etc.)?

After these questions are answered and organized in order of importance for your school, a timeline and a plan for building the schedule must be developed. Here's the scheduling process we used at Hatboro-Horsham High School:

1. First, we prepare the course selection guide (December/January). In early March, student assemblies are held to distribute course selection materials and explain the process. A one-night Curriculum Fair is held for parents that includes information booths staffed by teachers and informational meetings run by counselors.

2. Course selection
   - Students select courses (first 2 weeks of March)
   - Course selections are entered (end of March)

3. Tally prepared (early April)
   - Print course selection tally
   - Prepare sectioning of courses
   - Determine additional staff needed
   - Sectioning approved (second school board meeting in April)

4. Scheduling process
   - Special consideration lists from department chairs (mid-April)
   - Any special items from administrators
   - Prepare computer to build schedule (late April through May)
     a. Review directories used
     b. Determine how sectioning will be divided between semesters
     c. Enter sectioning into schedule builder
     d. Run schedule builder
     e. Schedule students
     f. Review results
     g. Repeat entire process until satisfactory schedule achieved

- Review completed schedule with department chairs (late May)
- Issue preliminary schedules to students (prior to final exams)

5. Preparation for school opening
   - Resolve conflicts with help of guidance counselors (before school ends)
   - Process new registrations (throughout the summer)
   - Assign homerooms and lockers (early July)
   - Assign study halls (early August)
   - Review class balancing (early to mid-August)
   - Mail schedules for students and teachers (third week of August)
   - Schedule problems to be handled by counselors (last week of August)
   - Print reports for teachers and counselors (day before opening)
     a. Class lists
     b. Study hall lists
     c. Locker lists
     d. Room schedules
     e. Homeroom lists
     f. Class tally

At this point, you must remember that the new time schedule will act as a catalyst that may affect several important areas of a school's infrastructure. Once you have a handle on your existing realities, you must decide which intensive scheduling alternative is best for you and your school community. There are no restrictions on what you can build. Be creative, and do not be afraid to develop new scheduling ideas that will better meet your program needs. After the key stakeholders decide which schedule is best, calculate the conversion rate. What will change? Where can we expect to see the most improvement? What will be affected positively or negatively? Typically, schools notice changes in the following areas (either pro or con), depending on which schedule is selected and how well it is implemented:

1. Staffing
2. Useable supplies and equipment for instruction, including textbooks
3. Technology use

4. Facility use
5. Class size
6. Professional development programs
7. School environment (discipline, stress, and learning)
8. Teacher and student performance inside the classroom
9. Teacher-made assessments
10. Attendance
11. Student achievement results (quantitative and qualitative)
12. Future plans of students

Be acutely aware that the contrast between intensive scheduling and traditional, assembly-line scheduling is significant. The traditional schedule is hectic, with a great deal of "start up" and "shut down." Adolescent students are asked to balance six to eight subjects per day and to deal with the same number of adult personalities. Teachers are asked to motivate and monitor 120 to 180 students from September until June while they prepare for five or six classes every day. The traditional period lends itself to passive instructional approaches, such as lectures, that ensure only coverage and that encourage memorization, not learning and utilization.

Conversely, intensive scheduling allows students to deal with only three or four subjects at a time, which allows for more focus and better learning. The longer blocks provide a better academic environment and encourage interactive methods, shifting teaching styles, and time for the application of concepts and skills. There is less stress for teachers and students alike, allowing for a more positive academic atmosphere. Intensive scheduling is more flexible and provides time for the core concepts as well as remediation and enrichment. Greater academic capacity and acceleration is also possible. The longer block opens the door for the integration of technology and a variety of quality assessments aligned with the curriculum. Most important, intensive scheduling allows teachers to deal with fewer students.

In Conclusion

I strongly believe that even the best schools can and will benefit significantly by making the move to intensive scheduling if the change process is followed as outlined earlier. Involvement, leadership, training, commitment, follow-through, and evaluation are all essential components that will ensure successful implementation.

While traveling across the nation visiting schools and discussing intensive scheduling, I am asked constantly to confirm which schedule is best. Once again, each individual school must make that decision. My personal favorites, however, are the 4 × 4 + 1 semester schedule and the nine-block trimester schedule. Both schedules provide wonderful academic learning environments and optimum flexibility that maximizes the capacity of the curriculum delivery system for students and teachers alike.

Another wave of time reconfiguration deals with organizing the school year as well as the school day. Schools are considering year-long schooling with mini-vacation breaks and intersessions for field trips, remediation, and enrichment. The goal is to have students involved with formal education throughout the year. Extending the school year, assuming the additional time is used effectively for instruction, is a powerful idea. Parents typically fight this initiative because it infringes on their personal family calendar, especially the traditional summer vacations. We need to realize, however, that the rest of the world's civilized nations routinely spend 200 days or more in school annually. Something has to give if we, as a nation, are to stay competitive in a global economy. Our system of education will clearly help determine the quality and productivity of our future workforce.

Some schools are tinkering with reorganizing the traditional 180-day school year as well. Two 75-day terms followed by a 30-day mini-term is a common example. Yet another creative approach is the 75-15-75-15 configuration. The mini-terms may be used for travel, field trips, special projects, school-to-work experiences, school for the arts, remediation, or enrichment. The 75-day terms may focus on the core curriculum and elective courses.

Educators must think creatively and look at time holistically as a change agent. The sky is the limit! Build a well-constructed educational package that, when delivered properly, will yield significant school improvement.

Now that you have decided on a block schedule, we must prepare teachers for the transition from traditional periods to a longer block of time. Chapter 3 will address professional development and teaching in an intensive schedule.

3

Preparing Teachers
for Intensive Scheduling

When intensive scheduling is implemented, we want to be sure that teachers are prepared to use the new time configuration more effectively. The primary goal is to build a site-based professional development model that will meet the needs of your staff. The model must provide teachers with the skills and competencies necessary to deliver the curriculum and other important academic experiences in a more interactive approach. Balance must be considered at every turn as we begin to look inside the intensive schedule. Curriculum balanced with skills, passive methodology versus active instructional strategies, textbooks versus software/CD-ROM, and traditional assessment versus performance-based approaches are just a few of the areas we need to fine tune. The intensive scheduling package must include a careful look at four key areas:

1. Curriculum
2. Instructional strategies
3. Technology utilization
4. Assessment

Although each school system must once again tailor the academic program to satisfy local needs, most successful schools strive to accomplish specific educational goals:

1. Create a schoolwide academic environment that is teacher and student friendly.
2. Emphasize student-centered classrooms.
   a. Project-based learning
   b. Thematic curriculum
   c. Exploratory learning
3. Personalize the academic program for every student (break schools into units of no more than 600 students).
4. Break classroom instruction into three basic approaches:
   a. Whole group
   b. Cooperative
   c. Independent
5. Shift instructional strategies at least three times per class using graphic organizers for planning and taking the seven multiple intelligences into account at all times.
6. Ensure that different teaching styles accommodate a variety of learning styles.
   a. Active versus passive
   b. Creative versus prescriptive
   c. Interactive versus independent
   d. Exploration versus receptivity
   e. Integration versus isolation
7. Seek interdisciplinary curriculum initiatives, and be sure to take the academic experiences beyond the borders of the school building.
8. Be sure to teach essential learnings and skills with proper pacing. Too many schools teach what the teachers like and are comfortable with instead of what is important for students to know. (Remember that a teacher's job is to ensure that learning takes place, not to ensure that material is covered.)
9. Make assessment a natural part of the daily academic flow and be sure it always aligns with the curriculum.

10. Provide quality time for enrichment, remediation, and cocurricular experiences.

So, where do we start the process of helping teachers make the transition to a longer block of time? I suggest we follow the same steps that took us from theory to practice in developing intensive scheduling.

1. Do a self-analysis. The professional development committee should create a site-based, anonymous survey that will ask teachers and students questions about the curriculum, instructional strategies, and individual teaching and learning styles.
2. Develop short-range expectations.
   a. Create a more interactive classroom.
   b. Improve student motivation.
   c. Improve student and teacher performance in the classroom.
   d. Integrate technology more frequently.
   e. Personalize the academic program for every student.
3. Establish a long-range vision.
   a. Create a 21st-century view of learning.
   b. Update the curriculum continually to meet the challenges that our students face now and in the future.
   c. Work toward every student and every teacher having a personal laptop computer that is part of a local area network and wide area network with easy Internet access.
   d. Improve student achievement results significantly.
   e. Evaluate teacher competencies constantly to ensure that the professional staff possess the skills and knowledge needed to do their jobs well.
4. Develop a plan and timeline that will take your staff from theory to practice.
   a. Build a site-based professional development program.
   b. Establish a professional development maintenance program for teachers who struggle with the transition.
   c. Develop a system of accountability that is fair and constructive to ensure improved instruction in the classroom.
5. Based on measurement and evaluation data, continue to update the professional development program.

It is important as we begin to build a professional development model that we take inventory of key areas:

1. Using the feedback from the self-analysis, assess teacher strengths and weaknesses from an instructional standpoint to determine where they need improvement.
2. Personalize your program. Not every teacher needs the same training. Steer away from a one-size-fits-all approach.
3. Require teachers to establish annual instructional goals and, more specifically, technology goals. Be sure you attach an accountability procedure for appropriate follow-up.

Another critical step in preparing for the actual implementation of teacher training requires each school system to establish clear-cut roles and skills for both the teacher and learner. Here is a typical example:

Teacher Roles and Skills

- Design opportunities for group interaction.
- Design debriefing activities to assess process.
- Center learning around students' interests and learning styles.
- Model a variety of information management strategies (plan, gather, organize, test, question).
- Decentralize responsibilities for learning to students.
- Act more like a coach—an idea planter and obstacle remover.
- Intervene in students' learning process with questions and cues.

Student Roles and Skills

- Is aware of process for learning; becomes a critical thinker and develops a process for learning
- Can manage information and apply it to appropriate situations
- Assumes increased responsibility for learning
- Is self-directed for life (6 to 10 career changes)
- Cooperates in group projects and collaborates in problem-solving situations
- Is an empowered planner with a rationale for organizing

These parameters for student and teacher performance must be created by all of the key stakeholders, keeping local priorities in mind but also using outside sources as a guide.

Let's turn now to the Hatboro-Horsham case study and examine how a site-based professional development model grew from self-analysis into successful intensive scheduling implementation inside the classroom. This model has been used by many schools in variations of the original theme.

Hatboro-Horsham High School started with an anonymous survey developed by the professional development committee, which established a list of strengths and weaknesses from both a schoolwide perspective and a personal teacher point of view. Goals and objectives for the training program were outlined clearly. Previous training workshops and retained competencies were considered as planning began. The final product had three basic components that eventually took my staff from theory to practice. Keep in mind that before our formal training activities started, a great deal of work took place by the administration and faculty leaders to ensure a positive professional attitude. Some mature staff members, negative thinkers, and complacent individuals needed attitude adjustments. Some required one-on-one meetings, whereas others needed to be "schmoozed" in some form. Nevertheless, we were ready to embark on the business of implementing our site-based intensive scheduling readiness program, which included three components:

1. All teachers became proficient at using cooperative learning techniques. Three-day workshops were designed and offered at a variety of times exclusively for high school teachers.

2. Teachers, administrators, students, and parents from schools already implementing intensive scheduling spoke to our staff about common concerns and positive experiences. All of the key stakeholders were involved in this experience. School visitations were also scheduled, and written reports were shared with everyone. Videotapes and conference calls were valuable in helping to answer specific questions and reduce anxiety.

3. Collaboration between classroom teachers and university professors took place. Dr. Robert Vogel and Dr. Preston Feden from LaSalle University facilitated a 4-day workshop for 20 teachers who were selected by their peers. The core group training, as

it was called, addressed the differences in how students learn and how teachers can best teach in a longer block of time. After the core group training was complete, these 20 teachers then trained the rest of the staff. The core group training program covered these key areas:

a. Graphic organization—ensures well-planned classroom experiences. Shifting methods, interactive strategies, integrating technology, and a variety of assessments were emphasized.

b. Teaching style/learning style—focuses on active instruction and how the brain works, including the seven multiple intelligences.

   i. *Logical-mathematical intelligence* deals with inductive and deductive thinking, numbers, and abstract patterns; sometimes called scientific thinking.

   ii. *Visual-spatial intelligence* relies on sense of sight and ability to visualize; includes ability to create mental images.

   iii. *Bodily-kinesthetic intelligence* relates to physical movement and the wisdom of the body; uses brain's motor cortex, which controls bodily motion.

   iv. *Musical-rhythmic intelligence* deals with recognizing tonal patterns, sounds, rhythms, and beats.

   v. *Interpersonal intelligence* has to do with person-to-person relationships and communication.

   vi. *Intrapersonal intelligence* relates to self-reflection, metacognition, and awareness of internal states of being.

   vii. *Verbal-linguistic intelligence* deals with words and language, both written and spoken.

c. Curriculum pacing and classroom management—ensures that as the block gets longer, there is more flexibility and uninterrupted time available. Teachers in the field consistently state that more coverage and learning is possible if efficient classroom management is present on a daily basis. Teachers need to become more competent at shifting methods and to be able to make smooth transitions that link together.

d. Technology integration—needs to be a daily occurrence, if possible. Technology needs to become as common in the classroom as a textbook. Teachers need to be trained first and have access to computer hardware and software.

e. Assessment and evaluation—means that teachers need to learn a variety of traditional and performance-based assessment methods. They also need to know when and how to deliver these assessments effectively.

f. Professional development maintenance—means that not all teachers, even after the training they receive, will be able to make a smooth transition and be successful initially. However, there are solutions:

   i. Assign a mentor.

   ii. Encourage collaborative planning and teaching.

   iii. Develop departmental sharing sessions.

   iv. Encourage interdisciplinary sharing groups.

   v. Monitor curriculum pacing and student results.

   vi. Record best and worst practices.

The following helpful steps should also be shared with struggling teachers:

Planning Phase

1. Focus in the core concepts of the course you are teaching. Using the principle "less is more," select broader concepts that will focus your instructional time by weeks.

2. Plan relevant activities around the major concepts. Develop a variety of activities. For each class period, plan a whole group activity, a partner or group concept, or a visual aid (i.e., video, filmstrip, movie, etc.).

3. Plan for different physical room arrangements. Rearrange the room for different kinds of activities. This helps keep students motivated through a fresh look from different perspectives.

Implementation Phase

1. Begin classes with advanced organizers. Advanced organizers are statements (oral and/or written) made by teachers just prior to presenting the day's lesson. These organizers help focus students' learning for the lesson, get them on the train,

and help them tap their prior knowledge to provide a scaffold for building new information.

2. Teach your students strategies for learning and organizing their knowledge. Encourage students to elaborate on their notes based on information you present to them in class. Use journals for a variety of reasons (i.e., self-reflection, elaboration, problem solving, etc.). Rather than always relying solely on linear strategies, teach them the use of graphic organizers to arrange key concepts and ideas in a different way.

3. Use a variety of learning environments during the input phase of your extended lesson.

   a. Whole group (lecture)

   b. Cooperative learning partners/groups

   c. Individual (journal writing, note taking, self-reflection)

4. Allow time and opportunity for students to practice using what they have been taught. Resist the temptation to move too quickly and focus only on facts. Present problems or scenarios for analysis by the students. Use consensus by groups to formulate answers to problems or scenarios. This allows you time to give feedback and constructive criticism to individuals and groups.

5. Projects and presentations are ways to ensure that pupils make information personally meaningful. After you have covered a core concept, allow students individually or in groups to expand on the concept by doing work that uses information and processes you have helped them master. Then, have them share and/or defend their work. This also allows you to broaden the scope of assessment.

There is no one correct way instructionally to thrive in an extended block of time. I have tried to present a variety of notions gathered from my experiences in working with students and teachers. The reminders mentioned above suggest that you should select core concepts, involve students in actively learning and applying concepts, vary the instructional activities to accommodate different learning styles, and broaden the scope of evaluation by including performance assessment.

Another piece of training that was created by the core group addressed substitute teachers. Early in September (before the staff gets sick), half a day of theory and half a day of observation took place for all commonly used substitutes. This helped prepare subs for life inside the block. This training, coupled with experience and support from colleagues, helped make this transition a smooth one.

Our overall site-based staff development plan took about a year and a half to complete. Most successful models take 1 to 2 years to implement. I was confident that my staff was well prepared, and I was right. We got off to a wonderful start, and the early reviews on the switch to intensive scheduling began pouring in after just 2 weeks into the first semester. As teachers got through the first quarter, then the first semester, and so on, the feedback became even better.

The key to ensuring success was communication and accountability. A quarterly newsletter was sent to parents that included anecdotal reports as well as empirical data. Parents, teachers, and students were anonymously surveyed on an ongoing basis. Most important, however, administrators and curriculum coordinators followed through with fair and constructive evaluation of the program. Although everyone knew that an annual evaluation instrument was in place that would compare 2 years of baseline data with 4 years of new information, it was the daily observations and communication with all of the stakeholders that kept the program on task. The following accountability steps were instituted:

1. Short but frequent classroom observations took place daily by the entire administrative staff. Most teachers were seen briefly on a weekly basis for the first 2 years of the new program. Administrators looked for those instructional initiatives that were committed to during the core group training.
2. Curriculum coordinators monitored curriculum pacing by collecting daily lesson plans. This was mutually agreed to by the teachers.
3. Best and worst practices journals were kept by each department.
4. Honor roll, attendance, and D and F grades were tracked and reported on a quarterly basis.
5. Students and teachers were informally surveyed about intensive scheduling at midyear during the first and second years.
6. Parents and students were encouraged to express concerns about intensive scheduling or isolated problems to teachers or administrators.

Let us focus specifically on classroom evaluation, which was administered by the principals and supervisors. It was agreed to during the core group training that administrative evaluation should take on a constructive and supportive tone. Only those teachers who did not prepare or who exhibited an unprofessional attitude would be subjected to disciplinary or punitive measures. Coordinators placed their emphasis on curriculum delivery and student achievement results. Administrators, on the other hand, focused on teacher and student performance in the classroom. Dr. Kevin Hart, formerly the principal at a nearby Montgomery County high school, built his doctoral thesis around the study of how intensive scheduling changes teacher behavior in the classroom. Our teachers took an anonymous survey after the first semester about how their teaching had changed. The surveys reflected an obvious trend from passive to active instruction. In addition, Hart's study shows significant movement toward more performance-based assessment.

The first step toward productive classroom evaluation under intensive scheduling starts by making sure that teachers have a clear understanding of what is expected. The expectations and main themes were outlined clearly during the core group phase of our professional development program as follows:

1. Be well organized daily.
2. Shift methods two to five times per block.
3. Get students engaged in their own learning.
4. Balance essential learnings with essential skills.
5. Integrate technology.
6. Balance traditional methods with interactive strategies.
7. Present key concepts and apply them to real-world situations.
8. Balance traditional assessments with performance-based evaluations.
9. Balance instruction evenly between whole group, independent, and cooperative approaches.
10. Do not lecture for more than 20 minutes at a time.

Four administrators divided 90 classroom teachers evenly for the first year. We rotated these groups each semester. Our goal was to spend an hour every morning and an hour every afternoon touring the building and visiting our group of teachers. Instead of spending the entire 85 minutes with one teacher, we spent 10 to 15 minutes per teacher. We tried to rotate our visits so that we would see different people at different times to ensure that the instructional expectations were being met. This technique worked well. We were visible in the building on a daily basis to students and faculty, which is always positive. We were able to give students and teachers ongoing support and constructive feedback through informal means. Our observations clearly reflected better planning, less lecture, and overall improved performance by the vast majority of staff members. The handful of teachers who were struggling or not meeting expectations were immediately confronted and placed into the professional development maintenance program. In 5 years, only two teachers met with serious problems when making the transition to intensive scheduling.

Last year, 98% of my teachers stated on our anonymous survey that they would not want to return to traditional scheduling. It is my opinion that the smooth transition we experienced at Hatboro-Horsham was clearly a result of our commitment to a well-planned professional development program that was built primarily by the teachers with help from outside sources. Remember, if they build it, they will come!

In Conclusion

Breaking Ranks: Changing an American Institution stated: "The school system should help educators to create a learning community in which substantive professional development, linked primarily to content knowledge and to instructional strategies, plays an ongoing part in their work" (NASSP, 1996, p. 62).

Professional development must be ongoing and remain after the key change is in place. Teachers need time for sharing, planning, and collaborating. This time needs to be stress-free if possible. Summer academies, retreats, and workshops outside of school are ways to ensure a flow of new ideas and provide needed refreshment. Commit to one change initiative at a time. Do not try to do too much all at once and clutter the professional platter. Clutter almost always leads to mediocrity or failure.

When I look back at that first September, as we approached 85-minute intensive blocks, I remember the teachers entering the building. They were nervous about what was going to happen, and the anxiety level was incredible. Despite the training, the reality of the situation was intimidating. My teachers were overprepared, carrying satchels full of materials and activities. The greatest moment for them was getting through the first week. Once they implemented intensive scheduling, they saw its positive potential almost immediately. With few exceptions, actually teaching in the longer block brought relief and satisfaction. As time went on, the classroom experience got better, and as a result, faculty commitment became stronger. When a positive student performance followed, it was easily the most rewarding time of their professional lives.

What followed was even more gratifying—national awards, a television appearance on "Good Morning America," and one partnership after another with businesses and higher education alike. Teacher grants and increased scholarship money for students flowed like never before.

The major fear after a success story like this is complacency. All of the key stakeholders must guard against falling back into the status quo. The key to sustaining the momentum of the program is ongoing measurement of student achievement results and teachers doing a competent job every day.

Let's look inside the classroom at how intensive scheduling affected teaching and learning in every subject area. Training is imperative, but proper implementation is the key to success. Chapter 4 will take a close look at teacher and student performance inside the newly constructed intensive schedule.

4

Teaching Inside the Block

Breaking Ranks: Changing an American Institution comments, "Responsibility for implementing instructional strategies ultimately rests in the hands of individual teachers who should prepare themselves well and be able to utilize a variety of strategies, in addition to lecturing, for effective student learning" (NASSP, 1996, p. 20). Clearly, teachers are empowered to engage students inside the classroom. The business of classroom management rests squarely on the shoulders of teachers. What is taught, how it is delivered, and the length of time spent on a particular concept are daily pedagogical decisions. Student motivation and academic progress are at least partially the instructor's responsibility. The quantity and quality of different assessments and the evaluation process are critical if educators are committed to both content coverage and student achievement. Assessment and evaluation need to guide the pace and direct the course of the educational program for every child. Both traditional and performance-based assessments need to be used and carefully aligned with the curriculum. Daily instruction and class assessments need to be part of a smooth flow of ideas, information, activities, demonstrations, and applications that meet the needs of each student. Portfolios, demonstrations, and projects need to become course requirements or mandated for graduation.

Classrooms need to become student centered. Teachers need to become coaches, facilitators, and partners in learning. Students need to become more actively engaged in their own learning. More important, students need to master critical competencies, including communication, problem solving, critical thinking, technology, and life skills. If these skills are mastered, students will become lifelong learners. In addition, learning will take place independently outside of the traditional classroom setting and without an instructor always leading the way. Students must learn *how* to learn.

Expectations for classroom interaction and results must be clearly outlined for students and teachers alike. Teachers must commit to shifting methods and using a variety of approaches. Sound traditional strategies should remain in the instructional mix and be matched with other complementary activities so that teaching styles accommodate learning styles. Efficient use of time and smooth transitions as methods shift will ensure greater time on task. A variety of physical room arrangements, technology integration, and subject matter mastery must also be in every teacher's satchel.

Assuming that teachers have the knowledge and skills they need to be successful, the factor that pulls it all together is planning. Teachers need more planning time because the longer block demands a more interactive and intensive approach to learning. Teachers who try to lecture too much, give students busywork, or simply double what they have always done in the past are doomed to failure. Teachers need to vary their approaches between whole group, independent, and cooperative experiences. Teachers need to think about what students need most, not what makes the teacher comfortable. Teaching the same way every day is unacceptable. Using a variety of interactive approaches, teachers need to achieve four basic goals during each block:

1. Gain the students' attention.
2. Present essential information.
3. Allow time for demonstration, practice, utilization, and/or application.
4. Take the class to a higher level using a creative technique or a stimulating activity. This step can also be used for assessment.

These four steps create a continuous cycle that should be implemented in a variety of ways. Teachers can follow different paths and still accomplish common instructional goals.

The impact of block scheduling on teachers across the nation has been remarkably consistent. Most teachers become better organized and begin to retool how they teach. The homework and assessment component improves in terms of quantity and quality. Homework becomes an extension of the classroom, and because students understand what happened in class, they are able to accomplish more at home. This entire homework-to-class-to-homework cycle radically improves efficiency, pacing, and results. Hatboro-Horsham developed a policy called Mandatory Remedial Homework (MRH), which required students to make up all assignments that were not turned in or not properly completed. Students have the option of reporting to study hall that afternoon or attending a Saturday morning 9:00 a.m. detention session for 2 hours. Students must hand in the homework the next day no matter which option they choose. Students who do not comply are suspended, and a parent conference is scheduled. MRH has drastically improved performance on homework assignments, but it has also increased cheating on homework. (Oh well, nothing is perfect!)

Attendance is another area that affects classroom instruction. If students are not present, it is difficult to teach them. The double periods often create anxiety among parents concerning attendance. They anticipate that 1 day of absence really becomes 2 days, which could create a double whammy effect. In reality, attendance typically stays the same in schools with high daily rates, and it often improves in schools with attendance problems. The longer block gives teachers the flexibility to help students make up work, and enhancement blocks are a wonderful solution for any remediation problems that may exist. Many schools implement tougher attendance policies when moving to intensive scheduling. At Hatboro-Horsham, we encourage a 20% participation grade. This grade includes in-class activities that cannot be made up or duplicated at any other time and places an emphasis on the importance of in-class activities. It always amazes me that so many students with a high percentage of absences can still obtain a grade of A or B. When this happens, it sends a terrible message to students and parents about the need to be prompt and on the job every day.

Student transfers may have a major impact on academic programming. Because not every school has made the transition to intensive scheduling, student transfers both incoming and outgoing present logistical hurdles, not roadblocks. Keep in mind that schools with assembly-line schedules already have dealt with differences in graduation requirements, credit values, sequential semester courses, and a variety of curriculum nuances. Which block schedule you select will determine which problems you face and also will lead you to the proper solutions. Remedial centers where tutoring can take place, as well as having 9-week and 18-week courses available, are just a few helpful solutions for transfers. Generic competency exams for each core curriculum area are also a helpful aid in assessing student progress and knowledge base. Most important, schools considering block scheduling need to talk to guidance counselors from similar schools already implementing intensive scheduling. Develop a list of ideas and helpful hints that can be used at your school to help student transfers experience a smooth transition.

Teacher accountability is another important area of concern. What happens when a teacher is unable or unwilling to make the transition to intensive scheduling? After every attempt has been made to help this teacher constructively, it is clear that dismissal is the only alternative. Although block scheduling improves the overall level of instruction drastically, there are at least one or two teachers who are not very good in the traditional environment, and block scheduling magnifies the problem. Typically, parents and students will take their worst traditional classroom experience involving a teacher and multiply times two. No matter what schedule you have at your school, incompetent, unprofessional teachers need to be confronted, corrected, or dismissed. Intensive scheduling forces all teachers to plan better, vary methodology, and lecture less. Those teachers who refuse to do this correctly will be more visible and easier to deal with under the intensive schedule.

Let's look at actual classroom instruction in each academic area. The academic disciplines are organized into three categories titled laboratory, other curriculum areas, and special education and advanced placement. We will analyze lessons from organizational, instructional, and curriculum perspectives. Please note that teachers tend to organize lessons in three basic organizational approaches:

1. By block (organize 80 to 120 minutes at a time)
2. By unit or segment of curriculum (could be spread over several blocks or days)
3. By concept (could be spread over several blocks or days)

All three lesson plan approaches are exhibited in Lessons A through H at the end of this chapter.

Laboratory Classes

This area includes science; family and consumer science (formerly home economics, textiles, and life skills courses); art; business; computer science; music; health and physical education; cooperative education (school-to-work opportunities); TV production; journalism; photography; architectural drawing (CAD, CAM); and vocational education. At the end of this chapter you will find lessons for art, child development, computer science, chemistry, language arts, trigonometry, government, and French. Please note, intensive scheduling allows all areas of learning to become more laboratory oriented at least some of the time. The areas mentioned above, however, are naturals for intensive scheduling. If necessary, science classes can have a lab experience every day, which provides for better continuity and a more efficient curriculum delivery system. Health and physical education have time to get students dressed, stretch, exercise, work on skills, participate in an activity, and assess all in one block! More important, physical education students start to take showers again. (Life is good!) These courses and curriculum areas are tailor-made for interactive educational experiences. The longer block allows more time for practice, application, and real-world connections that are critical to the success of these curriculum areas.

Other Curriculum Areas

English, math, social studies, and foreign language also benefit greatly from the longer block. The transition from traditional modes of teaching in these areas to a more interactive approach needs more planning and, in some instances, a break with conventional thinking. In English class, there is more time for writing, presenting, and interacting. Writing labs are more accessible, and time is available for acting out plays as well as educational trips to museums or the theater. The curriculum delivery process may be reorganized, and time spent on certain topics is often redistributed. How many poems do students need to read before they truly understand and appreciate the beauty of verse? How many Shakespeare plays must be read before this period of British literature is understood? Many English teachers spend inordinate amounts of time on literature they personally love when they could be spending more time on important communication skills. English teachers need to use the curriculum as a vehicle that moves students toward the application of language arts skills. Balance between content and skills is clearly the key to success. My observations have shown that many English teachers, more than in any other subject area, tend to view their content as sacred. These teachers have good reasons, I might add, because language arts skills are essential to the success of every person.

Math teachers have gained a reputation over the past 5 years of resisting the move to intensive scheduling. They often believe that sequential gaps are negative and that students can handle only one concept at a time. Methods like cooperative learning are often viewed as fluff and a waste of time. Interestingly, math teachers have been one of the easiest converts; once they experience intensive scheduling, they often become enthusiastic proponents. My math department was 100% against intensive scheduling in 1992. In 1997, the teachers champion the program. They report the ability to do everything they always did in the past but better. An improved homework experience, more technology use, and the ability to work with students individually or in small groups have had a positive impact on results. The Hatboro-Horsham math teachers have found that top students are achieving at the same level as before, but they see lower- and middle-ability groups flourishing. Coverage has remained about the same or has improved a little depending on the teacher. Teachers across the nation know now that efficient content coverage is clearly a product of classroom management, not scheduling.

My social studies department was one of the most enthusiastic about the move to intensive scheduling. In fact, they were disappointed that the blocks were only 85 minutes long. They went through the training, marched into the classroom, and lectured extensively! I realized at that point that the social studies department was excited about more time to talk about and discuss history. It took about 2 months to help make the adjustment to a more interactive approach. Interestingly, since the adjustment, the level of instruction has been outstanding and continues to improve on an ongoing basis.

Foreign language teachers could have qualified under the laboratory category. Typically, foreign language teachers love the longer block for instruction. Speaking, writing, interactive exchanges, and audio laboratory use make instruction a natural. The concern comes with the thought that serious foreign language students need to speak the language daily. At Hatboro-Horsham, we allow students to accelerate foreign language study (take each level in succession one semester after the other). I have also seen schools start culture clubs that meet before or after school or during enhancement time, where daily speaking takes place. Other schools employ the 3 × 3 + 2 schedule, which allows foreign language instruction to take place all year long. The option you choose is a local decision. Keep in mind that many schools do absolutely nothing additional and are happy with the foreign language delivery system and results.

Special Education and Advanced Placement Courses

Special education takes on a slightly different look from one state to the next. However, meeting the needs of gifted and challenged students, no matter which schedule you choose, is a formidable task. Remember that many schools place so much emphasis on addressing students with special needs that the children in the middle get lost in the shuffle. I strongly believe that schools should provide an individual educational plan or a personal plan of progress for every student in the system.

Intensive scheduling accommodates the desire to meet your special education program goals with great flexibility. No matter which block schedule you choose, the possibilities to better meet individual student needs are present. Acceleration, remediation, and enrichment opportunities abound. The gifted student usually finds greater academic capacity, which means that they can do more academically in a less stressful environment. I believe that the 4 × 4 scheduling concept is a wonderful model when considering special education. Teachers and parents have tremendous flexibility and numerous options when considering mainstreaming and resource room support. Students may take one or two mainstream classes per semester and spend the rest of the time getting support. If a student is mainstreamed for all classes, enhancement blocks provide a wonderful daily opportunity for support. The internal resource room schedule can follow the schoolwide block schedule or split blocks and develop rotations for team teaching possibilities. Gifted students can receive enrichment experiences by developing a rotating pullout schedule or during an enhancement block.

Another common occurrence for special education programs inside intensive scheduling involves staffing. Nationally, special needs students involved with intensive scheduling tend to take mainstream classes more often. Inclusion programs and collaborative teaching between regular education and special education teachers typically follows. This occurrence has taken place at my school and is viewed as extremely positive by all of the stakeholders.

Particularly, in the 4 × 4 semester model, advanced placement courses have been a source of controversy and debate. The Educational Testing Service has run some surveys on implementation and results. This effort, in my opinion, has been halfhearted and clearly not comprehensive enough. During the past 5 years, Hatboro-Horsham has received only two surveys. In both cases, there were some glaring questions not being asked about block scheduling. What type of block schedule is being used? Did your teachers receive adequate training? How was your schedule implemented? Did your school follow a well-planned process for change? Are all students required to take the advanced placement test? Does your school pay for each student to take the exam? How many weeks do you teach the advanced placement courses? Do you offer seminar classes that supplement the core instruction? How many students take advanced placement courses at your school?

As we all know, advanced placement courses are college-level classes. A score of 4 or 5 ensures college credit at most institutions of higher learning. In a school of 1,400 students, about 250 take advanced placement classes, which leaves 1,150 that do not! In addition, a 4 × 4 semester model closely resembles a college schedule. Double blocks for a semester is the same amount of time as one period a day all year long. The rub comes in two areas. A first semester advanced placement course ends in January, and those students are not tested until May. A second semester advanced placement course loses time because the Educational Testing Service requires testing to take place early in May. There are two obvious solutions. Offer 27-week advanced placement courses (Quarters 1, 2, and 3) or supplement the core blocks with seminar classes. Seminar classes can be offered as part of a split block or during an enhancement block.

At Hatboro-Horsham, we have almost doubled the number of students taking advanced placement courses since 1992 (presently, 200 of our students take advanced placement courses). In 1992, 52% of our students scored 3 or better on a 5-point scale (5 is the highest score possible). By the way, we pay for the test and require that every student take it. In 1997, 67% of our students scored 3 or better, and more important, we had the highest percentage ever score a 4 or a 5. These types of results are typical from schools that have built their schedule properly and have addressed advanced placement classes as a priority. In my opinion, the Educational Testing Service finds block scheduling inconvenient from a business perspective. They simply do not want to offer testing at midyear and again in May. If this is the case, I wish that the Educational Testing Service would simply state its position instead of unfairly pointing the finger at intensive scheduling as a possible negative concerning advanced placement results. Go beyond the corporate rhetoric and talk to schools like yours about advanced placement instruction and results. I know you will hear a different side of the story.

In Conclusion

Intensive scheduling provides new instructional opportunities for teachers and students. Creating greater flexibility and more uninterrupted time on task increases the potential for improved student and teacher performance. The key, however, is for teachers and students to realize this newfound potential and act on it daily. Proper classroom management, student motivation, and high expectations are still critical factors that must be present for schools to be truly successful and improve significantly. Teacher training and student readiness are needed to ensure success. Fair and constructive teacher and program evaluation is imperative.

There is no perfect time schedule. However, I believe that intensive scheduling is a better alternative than traditional scheduling. At Hatboro-Horsham, the most impressive benefit from intensive scheduling has taken place inside the classroom. By changing our time schedule, we transformed the teaching and learning process from passive to active. I am most proud of how we restructured the learning environment and improved both instruction and results. If the people inside your organization use the new schedule as a helpful tool and commit to a new and better instructional approach, the students will be the ultimate winners.

Let's review examples of actual teacher lesson plans developed specifically to use the instructional benefits of longer blocks of time. The following lessons, labeled A through H, should be examined from organizational, instructional, and curriculum perspectives.

FROM THE ART DEPARTMENT

- "Intensive scheduling enables us to cover aesthetics, art history, and studio (application) in one class period."
- The following lesson when taught during the 45-minute class was fragmented and lacked continuity--this lesson would have taken 3 periods.

UNIT: OPTICAL ILLUSIONS

Day 1

- 10 min.   AESTHETICS: GROUP DISCUSSIONS
  Students group in fours and list optical illusions in nature and society including perspectives of tracks and highways. Class discussion and examples are provided.

- 20 min.   Art History: (lecture)
  1.   View and introduce various types of illusions; illusion of depth and contrast
     HAND OUT "ART ILLUSIONS"
  2.   STUDENTS APPLY THE TYPES OF ILLUSIONS TO MAJOR WORKS OF ART
  3.   INTRODUCTION TO OPTICAL ART MOVEMENT: 1964
     U.S., ENGLAND, AND FRANCE
     Definition of the art
     ARTISTS: VASARELY, ALBORS, STELLA

- 30 min.   APPLICATION STUDIO:
  MINI PROJECT: ART GRID SHEET
  Exercise using markers to create a grid optical illusion (illusion of contrast and illusion of depth)

- 10 min.   STUDIO:
  Introduce major project/ search for ideas

Lesson A: Art Major II lesson plan

SUBJECT/COURSE: Child Development
LESSON TOPIC: Enhancing Children's Self-Esteem

Introduction (10 Minutes)

1. A recording of "The Greatest Love" by Whitney Houston is played. A brief
    discussion elicits the fact that "the greatest love of all" is learning to love
    yourself, i.e., self-esteem.
2. Students read and discuss the "Peanuts" cartoon.

Body of Lesson

1. Fifteen-minute video -- "Mirrors: A Film About Self-Esteem," free-loan
    video from Modern
2. Five- to ten-minute discussion
3. Twenty-minute activity -- "Building Johnny's Self-Esteem"

    Each student is given an index card. On one side is a positive phrase,
    which would build self-esteem; on the other side is a negative phrase,
    which would demean the child. As each student reads the positive
    phrase, on a large "paper-doll" cutout figure of "Johnny," teacher writes a
    positive feeling that this would create. When all are read, Johnny feels
    proud, safe, loved, independent, etc. Then, as each student reads the
    negative phrase from the cards, the teacher snips and cuts the Johnny
    figure with scissors. Johnny is "cut up."

Follow-Up/Conclusion (Remaining Time)

Students complete a worksheet of what they could say or do in various situations
to enhance the child's self-esteem. Can be done in pairs or small groups or
completed for homework if time runs out or situations on worksheet could be
role-played.

Lesson B: Sample lesson plan for intensive scheduling 90-minute classes

I. Objectives
    A. Students will be able to apply their previous study of computer architecture in order to compare two different computer systems.
    B. Students will learn to scan an image.
    C. Students will be able to use applied learned document formatting techniques to enhance their documents.

II. Methods
    A. From computer magazines, students will select two computer systems to compare.
    B. Teacher will demonstrate to each student, individually, how to use the scanner, while other students begin their comparisons.
    C. By following the attached instructions, students will complete their project on their own.

III. Resources
    A. Scanner
    B. At least one computer magazine per student
    C. Computer lab with computers and printers available
    D. MSWord

IV. Evaluation
    A. Grades will be assigned to the final project using the following criteria:
        1. Adherence to directions
        2. Quality of computer system summaries
        3. Logic and criteria used to choose between two computer systems
        4. Document formatting, appearance, and creativity
        5. Focus and diligence of work during the class period

Attached documents:
    Instructions to students
    Sample outcome

Lesson C: Buying a computer project: Sample intensive/block schedule lesson plan, Hatboro-Horsham High School

Topic: Bonding

Valence Shell Electron Pair Repulsion Theory

Objective: Upon completion of the reading laboratory work and problems, and
               when asked to demonstrate their understanding either orally, using
               models, or on a written test, students will (a) explain how the
               shared and unshared pairs of electrons determine the molecular
               shapes of simple covalently bonded electrons and (b) predict the
               shapes and bond angles of simple molecules using the VSEPR
               theory.

Theory: The VSEPR theory states that because all electron pairs repel,
               molecules adjust their shapes so that the valence-electron pairs
               are as far apart as possible.
               Multiple bonds act as one center of electron density.
               Electron pair repulsions are not always equal. They can be ranked
               as follows:
                         Strongest: two unshared pairs
                         Moderate: one unshared pair and one shared pair
                         Weakest: two shared pairs

Methods: Using dot diagrams, actual models of the various shapes will be
               developed for two through six pairs of electrons. Each shared pairs
               will be replaced by lone pair(s), and the resulting effect on shapes
               and bond angles will be discussed. The appropriate name and
               sketch will be reviewed.

               Students will work in groups of two using actual models to build
               and determine the appropriate geometries.

Further development: Students will be asked to predict the effect of the geometry
               on simple molecules that contain polar covalent bonds. This
               material will be turned in for review and evaluation by the teacher.

Materials: Molecular model kits
               Overhead masters
               Laboratory--Covalent Molecule
               Computer Program on VSEPR theory designed by student for
               practice

Lesson D: Chemistry lesson plan

I.   Vocabulary Presentation (approx. 20 minutes): Entire class has been assigned a vocabulary unit to be completed for this period. One particular "TRIAD" has also been assigned the task of reviewing the practice exercises in the form of some competitive game. They will conduct, review, and score all the class "TRIADS" during the review lesson. The triad with the most points will be exempt from that week's quiz.

II.   Introduce New Piece of Literature: CYRANO DE BERGERAC

    A. BACKGROUND AND LITERARY TERMS
       Students will take notes on their review sheets as we play "OPRAH." OPRAH introduces each of the major characters.

    B. Selected students will be given cue cards for their responses to questions.

    C. Teacher plays "OPRAH," asking pointed questions regarding the important background information needed on each character before reading.

    D. In pairs, students compare notes taken during the character responses by their classmates, making certain they have grasped all important concepts.

    E. Teacher discusses style and setting of play.

    F. Begin reading; may be aloud or with cassette of play.

III.   Discuss writing a characterization: Sample thesis statements are generated aloud and put on board. Students select one and may be assigned the writing of a characterization for homework. They are to select any major character met in today's reading selection. (This paragraph will be edited again and additions made when play is finished.)

Lesson E: Sample language arts lesson based on an 85-minute period class: Seniors: College bound

1.   Have students finish presenting their graphs to class. (Students had
      worked on graphing variations of trigonometric functions other than sin x
      and cos x in pairs and were presenting their graphs with explanations to
      the class. Three presentations were done today:
            $y = -3 + 2\csc x$
            $y = \tan (1/2)x$
            $y = \tan x + \cot x$

(10 minutes)

2.   Introduction of logarithms:

      Def: The logarithm to a given base of a positive number is the exponent
      that indicates the power to which the base must be raised in order to
      obtain the number.

Using the definition given, finish the following:

$\log_2 8 = ?$

Discuss solutions--give justification for your response

"The logarithm to base b of N is L" is written:

$\log_b N = L$

Alternate definition: $\log_b N = L$ if and only if

$b^L = N$; $N > 0$, $b > 0$, $b \neq 1$

Ex. Write $\log_4 64 = 3$ in exponential form.

(Class does--verify on overhead)

Ex. Write $81^{1/2} = 9$ in logarithmic form.

(Class does--verify on overhead)

NOTE: The logarithm may be integral, fractional, or irrational.

Lesson F: Trigonometry lesson plan

NOTE: Since $b^0 = 1$, then $\log_b 1 = 0$
Since $b^1 = b$, then $\log_b b = 1$
If $a^n = a^m$, then $n = m$.

Ex. Find N if $\log_5 N = 3$
Ex. Find b if $\log_b 64 = 2$
Ex. Find a if $\log_{64} 4 = a$

(Notes, examples, and explanations are done on the overhead with time for student to try problems and then check work. Use overhead to give example-- shut off light so student can try the problem while you write it down--then turn light back on when majority are finished so everyone can see if they did the work correctly but still have an opportunity to try work on their own.)

(15 minutes)

3.   Have students go to the board (all if you have board space or half at time with rest working at seats.) All do the same problems. This gives teacher an opportunity to see everyone working at the same time. Students get used to helping one another when they get used to working at the board. There is a great deal of sharing ideas with this activity. It allows the teacher to direct attention to a problem solved in a clear and correct manner.

Find L if: 1. $\log_2 16 = L$
2. $\log_8 4 = L$
3. $\log_3 1/27 = L$

Find N if: 1. $\log_3 N = 4$
2. $\log_{16} N = 3/4$
3. $\log_5 N = -4$

Find b if: 1. $\log_b 343 = 3$
2. $\log_b 16 = 4$
3. $\log_b 9 = 2/3$

(20 minutes)

4.   Have students work on the following worksheet. Work individually. If you are really having difficulty you may check with your partner for verification

Lesson F: Trigonometry lesson plan, continued

or help. Turn in as you finish. You may take a two-minute break as you finish.

(15 to 20 minutes)

5.   As you return from your break and as the people in your base groups finish the worksheet, get in your base groups to do the following:

Read the properties of logarithms on pp. 397-398. Study examples. Discuss the properties with the members of your group. Put into your notes the verbal and mathematical statements for the logarithm properties of products, quotients, and powers. Study the examples given.

Base groups 1 and 4 are responsible for introducing the logarithm property of product.
Base groups 2 and 5 are responsible for introducing the logarithm property of quotient.
Base groups 3 and 6 are responsible for introducing the logarithm property of powers.

One person will be randomly called on tomorrow from each pair of base groups to give a presentation to the class. You will be graded on the same rubric as your last presentation. Anyone observing an error and able to correct it will be given points toward their presentation score.

(20 minutes)

6.   Homework: p. 398 # 1-27 odd, # 29-52 all. Finish any preparation needed for class presentations tomorrow.

Lesson F: Trigonometry lesson plan, continued

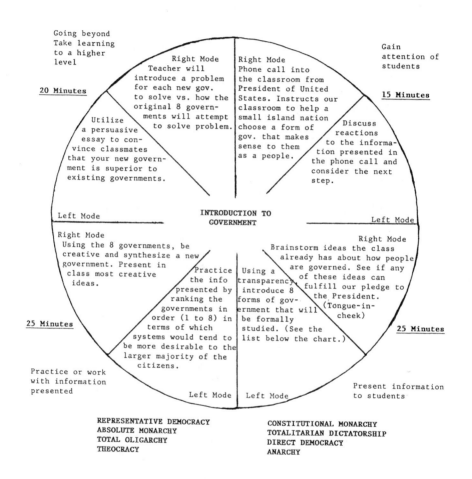

Lesson G: Sample government lesson plan

This lesson plan is typical of one that might be used for an 85-90 minute class period. The key to planning for this length of time is to use several different activities. It is best to try to think in terms of 15-20 minute segments for each activity.

I.   WARM-UP: (10 minutes) I like to use this as a quick oral review of such things as numbers, days of the week, months, weather expressions, classroom objects, colors, what students are wearing, etc.

II.   ORAL PRACTICE WITH THE OVERHEAD PROJECTOR: (15 minutes) Prepare an overhead transparency to practice structures that were taught in the previous class period. Some examples: regular and irregular verbs, converting statements to questions, making sentences negative, the infinitive construction.

III.   HOMEWORK: (20 minutes) This is an important part of the lesson plan. I like to send the students to the board to write their homework exercises. This serves as a kind of break because it gets the students out of their seats. Before sending a student to the board to write, he or she must first read the sentence aloud. If it is incorrect, he or she is given the opportunity to make corrections before writing it up, and the other students are able to give input as well. While the students are at the board, I can go around and make note of those who have not done their assignment or have not completed it. We then go over the answers as they appear on the board.

IV.   TEACHING NEW MATERIAL: (20 minutes) If the new material is vocabulary, I like to use the overhead transparencies that accompany the text. Whenever possible, I like to bring in previously learned vocabulary to lead up to the new. If the new material to be taught is a structure, I like to introduce it orally and have students practice orally before writing it on the board. I always encourage students to copy the new structure off the board, even though it might be written right in the text. This helps them remember it.

V.   PAIRED PRACTICE: (10-15 minutes) Students use their texts to practice a dialog in pairs. This might be using the structure that they have just learned or one that was learned in another class period. While they are practicing, I go around and listen or I sometimes team up with a student if there is an uneven number.

Lesson H: Sample French I lesson plan

When students have gone through all the dialogs, I choose a different pair of students to perform each dialog for the whole class.

VI.   LISTENING QUIZ: (5-10 minutes) Usually not announced beforehand. It might be something on numbers. Example: I will say a number in French and I want you to write the numeral that comes directly after (or before). Another type of quiz that I often give involves vocabulary. Students are told that they will hear a statement followed by a question. If the answer to the question is logically yes, write a plus sign. If the answer is logically no, write a minus sign. Example: Paul fait la grasse matinee. Est-ce qu'il est dans sa chambre? (Paul is sleeping late. Is he in his room?)

VII.   CLOSURE AND ASSIGNMENT: (5-10 minutes) Briefly go over the new structures or vocabulary that have been presented during the class and hand out the assignment or write the page numbers and exercises on the board, if it is a book assignment.

This is just a sample of a lesson plan. Other activities that I often use are videos, slides, songs, and games. We also have a language lab which we use twice a week for 45 minutes at a time. Group activities involving 3 or 4 students can be done as well. Students can practice dialogs or develop their own skits when they are ready. The 85-minute block has not been a problem as far as filling the time is concerned. I would like to mention that I never give my students time in class to work on homework. Homework is to be done outside of class. I believe that the time in class should be spent as much as possible doing listening and speaking activities. I always wait until the end of the period to make the assignment.

Lesson H: Sample French I lesson plan, continued

5

Impact on
Curriculum and Technology

We live in a complex, fast-moving computer age. There are few avocations or daily routines that do not require the use of technology in some way. Computers are replacing traditional functions at home, work, or play. Banking, entertainment, investing, shopping, communicating, and information gathering are all common-place occurrences.

Integrating a variety of technologies into the curriculum and instruction techniques are a must for all schools at every level. The computer and all the related hardware create a critical mass that every student must be able to access on a consistent basis. The ongoing use of technology must be as routine as the textbook, paper, and pencil. Before students will have open access to technology in the classroom, their teachers must be knowledgeable, comfortable, and competent with the use of the critical mass. The key to ensuring open access and quality utilization is a well-coordinated 3- to 5-year plan. At Hatboro-Horsham, our school board, headed by an experienced business person named Daren Miller, made a tremendous commitment to a 5-year technology plan. A bond issue was floated to provide inservicing, and CELT (The Center for Educational Leadership and Technology, out of Massachusetts) was contracted as an outside consultant to construct a blueprint that met our instructional technology needs. The plan had four core themes:

1. Produce adequate infrastructure (wiring, cables, etc.) for every school, including local area and wide area networks. This also includes your own Internet node.
2. Provide students and teachers with adequate critical mass (computers, printers, televisions, CD-ROMs, and all related software packages). Each school system needs to commit to a realistic student-to-computer ratio (one computer for every four students or four computers in every classroom, etc.).
3. Adequate teacher training must take place on an ongoing basis. Once again, critical mass must be available for teachers to use. If the teachers are not comfortable and competent with technology applications, these practices will never reach the classroom. At Hatboro-Horsham, we purchased a laptop computer for *every* professional employee. Additional workdays were built into the contract for the purpose of training. The training covered a variety of topics and levels that were offered primarily on inservice days and throughout the summer on a sign-up basis. Teacher competencies were developed, and training was personalized to meet individual needs. Every professional employee was required to set an annual technology goal, and accountability procedures were established to ensure successful completion.
4. Student technology competencies must be developed and integrated into every curriculum area. The use of technology as an instructional tool should not be an exclusive event. Technology use should be part of the daily instructional practices, such as writing, calculating, presenting, organizing, or gathering information.

Remember, like time, technology acts as a catalyst in the classroom. It provides an interactive instructional tool for students to access. It allows for hands-on exploration and may stimulate all of the seven multiple intelligences.

At Hatboro-Horsham, we have identified the following secondary teacher competencies:

1. Basic Windows 97
2. PowerPoint

3. Integrade (student grade book)
4. Excel
5. Internet usage
6. Printshop
7. Content-specific software applications
8. Access

Here is an overview of the secondary student technology program:

1. Every student must take keyboarding/word processing by Grade 6.
2. Every middle school classroom will have four computers and two printers for student use. There are three supplementary labs available. The creative arts rotation offers a hands-on technology lab that has seven different stations.
3. Introduction to computer applications or an approved replacement (based on demonstrated competency levels) is a graduation requirement at the high school.
4. The computer science department offers a variety of electives, including advanced placement computer science.
5. At the high school, there will be four computers and two printers in every classroom for student use, and there are five supplementary computer labs available.
6. There will be a local area network (LAN) and wide area network (WAN) as well as open Internet access throughout the middle school and high school.
7. Daily attendance and student records will be completed directly through the classroom computer.

Technology should be present and is necessary in every school no matter what time schedule you employ. Intensive scheduling, however, provides a more flexible instructional environment that encourages technology use and makes it easier to do. How often have you heard teachers in the assembly-line schedule say, "I wish I could do more with technology, but I just cannot find the *time*."

The hectic start-up and shut-down realities of the traditional classroom experience make anything other than lecture or limited discussion difficult to manage. The assembly-line schedule encourages an emphasis on coverage, memorization, and passive methodology, not active learning.

Technology has made a positive impact on curriculum development and instructional strategies in our schools. Giving teachers and students access to the information superhighway has transformed how educators plan and deliver the curriculum. Traditional textbooks will certainly remain in place but will not be the only source of information. As we approach the next century, our students will need to be knowledgeable in these areas:

1. Internet access
2. Software applications
3. Textbook information
4. Mass media access
5. Global economic factors
6. Higher education research

Although these six areas may overlap, each one is essential in developing a student's knowledge base. In general, content and information are growing so rapidly, they are impossible to harness, and this has created heated debates over what will drive our curriculum in the future. Some educators believe that textbooks may someday become obsolete. The role and inner workings of libraries (or media centers) have already changed radically over the past 10 years. Lack of regulation and credibility make the Internet an unstable but terribly exciting source of information and communication.

Intensive scheduling will not dictate curriculum changes. It does, however, provide a new and exciting learning environment that may affect what is being taught. At Hatboro-Horsham, we made a conscious effort to keep our curriculum the same. We did this because our evaluation tool was set up to measure the results on standardized final exams before and after intensive scheduling. After the first year, my teachers expressed the desire to make adjustments to the curriculum. They saw the opportunity to do a better job with the overall instructional delivery system. Interdisciplinary approaches, collaborative teaching, performance-based assessment, and the integration of technology were just a few of the doors that started to open.

So, how does a school identify the essential learnings? What do those 23 million new jobs that experts talk about look like? How do we get our students ready for the global economy? What challenges will the 21st century hold for today's youth?

1. Develop a 3- to 5-year curriculum cycle.
2. Allow teachers to build the curriculum within mandated guidelines.
3. Identify skills, challenges, and learnings that students will need in the future to be successful in these key areas:
   a. Work
   b. Higher education
   c. Family life
   d. Citizenship
4. Have each organizational segment (departments) in your school address 21st-century challenges from its own perspective. Each academic area should then build solutions and applications into the curriculum that will help students be better prepared for life.
5. Be sure that your time schedule and classroom management techniques put teachers and students in the best possible learning environment.

In Conclusion

I have a major concern that too many schools view technology as a quick and easy way to improve student achievement results. Technology, like time, will not transform results in isolation. The change process, curriculum, instruction, resources, training, and technology need to be molded into the right educational package that works for your school.

I have seen schools invest millions of dollars in technology with no organized plan for use or implementation in the classroom. Administrators and school boards must assume the responsibility for the planning phase. Administrators also need to lead by example. If necessary, get involved in the technology training workshops. Establish an internal administrative computer system that will handle student records, attendance, grade reporting, and scheduling. Technology should be both flexible and effective in helping schools manage information.

Curriculum, instructional strategies, and technology must complement each other and work in concert. The curriculum must be accurate and efficient. Ideally, we must strive to teach essential concepts that relate closely to real-world applications. If students can see these relationships, connections, and applications, and realize the importance of each learning experience, intense motivation often follows.

When sound curriculum is delivered in an interactive way and meshed with skills and technology integration, the classroom environment comes alive with excitement. The formula for success is clear. If we build the educational package as outlined and consistently follow through in the classroom, educators have an excellent opportunity to improve schools and student achievement results.

6

Evaluation and Results

Even before you begin implementation of intensive scheduling, a systematic plan for measuring the impact of your key change is imperative. A baseline study of at least 1 year (I prefer 2 years so that a baseline average can be developed) compared to 2 to 4 years of a new scheduling program is suggested. Both quantitative and qualitative data should be gathered and analyzed. An evaluation committee with representation from all the key stakeholders should handle the evaluation process independently without interference from administrative or governing bodies.

Consistent communication of short-term and long-term results is important. Quarterly or biannual newsletters sent home with report cards and offering both anecdotal experiences and empirical data is a very positive technique. The annual study should be shared with all of the key stakeholders and be presented publicly in a credible and professional manner.

Collaboration between local schools and doctoral dissertations or university research projects is another successful approach. In addition to our own internal study at Hatboro-Horsham, we have had two doctoral dissertations focus on our intensive scheduling program. Dr. Kevin Hart explored the impact that time change made on teacher and student performance inside the classroom. Dr. John Cornelius surveyed 24 schools in a variety of quantitative and qualitative categories. Outside independent studies combined with your own internal evaluation are a powerful way to sustain the reform initiative, and they also will open the door for the next key change.

Unfortunately, in some communities, even credible evaluation tools and positive reliable data fail to sway the political winds. I was recently sent a university study that is one of the most impressive I have ever seen. The results from an election created a new board majority that was against the 4×4 semester schedule, which had been implemented the year before. Despite the overwhelming data supporting the success of the new schedule, the board voted to arbitrarily install an alternating-day block eight schedule. The moral of this true story is clear: Sometimes, we confuse people with the facts! More important, keep politics free of educational priorities, because they seldom mix well.

Let us turn our attention to two examples of credible internal and external evaluation tools. First, at the end of this chapter in Appendix 6-A you will see the Hatboro-Horsham 6-year study in its entirety. Please note that in Year 7 (1996-1997 school year results are not part of the 6-year study), we continued to watch our results improve. SAT results, final exams, final grades, PSAT results, and advanced placement scores all increased slightly. This internal quantitative and qualitative study was developed by a committee of 23 people. Four people— Dr. Dorothy Kueny, science department chairperson; Sue Lyons, reading specialist; Peg Kleppinger, librarian; and school board member Dr. Jim Hessinger—spearheaded the formulation and yearly follow-up on this study.

The second example is the following discussion of an external study, which is part of a doctoral dissertation completed by Dr. John Cornelius (1997), Assistant Principal at Hatboro-Horsham High School. John's perspective was interesting because he could compare his own successful experience 4 years into intensive scheduling with 24 other schools on a variety of pressing questions and statistical areas.

Because Dr. Cornelius's study is 174 pages long and includes more than 60 pages of hard data, it is not possible to include all of the information in this book. The analysis of results and evaluations on a variety of block schedules from a national perspective may be a topic of interest in the future. Higher education research studies, as well as state governmental studies, are starting to appear. For example, the Department of Education in Virginia is in the process of concluding a comprehensive statewide study on block scheduling. Credible data are badly needed to help sustain the momentum of intensive scheduling as a viable school reform initiative. Studies that are developed by individual schools, although essential, are too narrow and isolated when we try to identify sweeping positive or negative trends.

Dr. Cornelius's study, which can be obtained by contacting him directly, surveyed all of the key stakeholders on some of the most often-asked questions about intensive scheduling. The 24 schools involved included 23 4 × 4 semester schedules and one alternating-day block 8 schedule. The purpose of the study was to answer four research questions:

1. What are the characteristics and structural features of intensive scheduling as they are being implemented in American high schools?
2. What are the similarities and differences among the programs?
3. What are the perceptions of staff, students, and administrators about the strengths and weaknesses of their intensive scheduling program?
4. What are the similarities and differences in perceptions found among individuals at the schools surveyed?

To answer these questions, a survey was conducted using two questionnaires constructed specifically for this purpose.

Design of the Questionnaires

The questions in this survey were designed to elicit information concerning the characteristics and components of the various schools' intensive scheduling programs. The actual survey questions used were based on important issues relating to intensive scheduling identified in the literature, as well as the researcher's experience with intensive scheduling. The questions were felt to be both relevant and appropriate for collecting the data necessary to answer the study's research questions.

General Questionnaire

The survey package included a 25-item questionnaire addressed to one administrator, two teachers (typically, the heads of the English and mathematics departments), and five students (the presidents of the junior and senior classes and student council, a special education student, and one student of lower academic ability) from each school. It gathered data on the respondents' perceptions regarding the strengths and weaknesses of their intensive scheduling program. Issues covered by these questions included reduction of stress, active learners, faculty and student morale, retention of knowledge, variety of teaching strategies, improvement in grades, preference for an intensive program, impact on at-risk students, and discipline problems.

These eight categories of respondents were selected for the general questionnaire because the researcher felt that they represented a cross section of the school population and were stakeholders in the intensive scheduling versus traditional education issue.

Department heads were chosen from English and mathematics, rather than from the similar fields of science and mathematics or English and social studies. The researcher selected the three student organization presidents because he felt that they were qualified to present their perceptions on the strengths and weaknesses of their intensive scheduling program. Because many critics of intensive scheduling feel that the program may be harmful to special education or lower-ability students, one student from each of these categories was selected to participate in the study. The researcher also felt that these five students would represent the full range of student ability levels. The administrator was also included in this questionnaire because administrators are the primary stakeholders in any change in school policy.

In selecting the topics for the general questionnaire, the researcher relied upon his experiences with Hatboro-Horsham's intensive scheduling program as well as his familiarity with the issues in the intensive scheduling versus traditional education debate gained from discussions with many administrators, teachers, students, parents, and school board members around the United States.

The questionnaire solicited information on topics that a number of the educators and researchers cited in Chapters 1 and 2 have stressed are related to the successful education of students in the United States. By considering all of the sources above for topics and issues related to intensive scheduling, the researcher was able to design a general questionnaire that was reasonably thorough and complete in its coverage of the issues.

The topics covered in the questionnaire can be broken into four basic categories:

1. *Classroom goals*—These are the major goals that educators and researchers agree are essential for improving the classroom learning environment. These topics include active learning, higher-order thinking skills, personalizing relationships, learning rather than memorizing, and the use of a variety of teaching and learning strategies.

2. *Secondary classroom goals*—These goals included questions on stress, morale, ability to concentrate, class discussions, and completing homework.

3. *Major issues*—These topics were central to the debate of intensive scheduling versus traditional education and included retention of learning, at-risk students, schedule conflicts, reduction of class size, teacher lectures, discipline problems, student grades, and effects on student ability levels.

4. *Intensive scheduling versus traditional education*—Five questions asked respondents to directly compare or judge their previous traditional schedule with their current intensive schedule.

In all four categories, the five respondents were extremely positive about intensive scheduling and clearly favored their block schedule over the traditional alternatives. The general questionnaire strongly supports the trends established from my data and experiences with intensive scheduling nationally.

Administrator Questionnaire

An additional 23-question survey answered only by administrators gathered descriptive, factual information that identified characteristics of each program relating to issues such as drop-out rate, SAT/ACT scores, attendance rate, course failures, discipline referrals, program modifications since inception, staff development and inservicing, program implementation, instructional strategies, program costs, and negative aspects of the program. Because the survey was intended to collect only factual data, it was deemed sufficient that only one administrator from each school answer the questions.

Question 1 asked the schools to summarize the characteristics of their intensive scheduling model, including the number of periods in a school day, the length of the class period, and duration (in weeks) of the classes offered. Questions 2 through 6 covered trends in dropout rate, SAT/ACT scores, attendance, course failures, and discipline referrals. The responses provided the data necessary to accurately compare the success of the schools' intensive scheduling programs with their former traditional programs. The results overall were extremely positive in favor of intensive scheduling for all of these areas.

Questions 7 through 9 solicited information on the problems that the schools had encountered in establishing their intensive scheduling program, as well as modifications under consideration or already implemented. Questions 10 through 21 provided data on courses, implementation needs, teaching load, staff development, start-up costs, and instructional strategies.

Question 22 addressed a major concern of guidance personnel: students transferring from traditional programs to an intensive scheduling school, and the problems the students might face. Question 23 requested the administrators' views of how intensive scheduling has affected their special education students—an issue often raised by critics of intensive scheduling.

Sample for the Survey

A list of 150 high schools thought to be employing intensive scheduling was compiled from a variety of sources, including listings by the Metropolitan Educational Research Consortium at Virginia Commonwealth University, the Pennsylvania Association of Secondary School Principals, magazine articles, books, and school names given to the researcher through his contacts with schools around the country that have implemented intensive scheduling programs. Surveys were sent to these 150 schools. In an effort to alert some of the schools to the upcoming study, the researcher also telephoned approximately 20 of the schools personally.

Unfortunately, only 24 schools were able to participate in the study. These schools are located in Virginia, Pennsylvania, Maryland,

Alabama, North Carolina, South Carolina, and Colorado. Although the researcher had hoped for a much better response, it is possible that the requirements of completing two surveys of 23 and 25 questions each discouraged many of the schools from participating. This low response rate is obviously a major limitation of this study.

All 24 participating schools completed the 25-question general questionnaire (addressed to administrators, teachers, and students). Of those 24 schools, 21 administrators also completed the 23-question administrator questionnaire (addressed to administrators only). Neither survey obtained a 100% response rate to every question.

Significance of the Study

Our traditional, concurrent scheduling system of high school education has received much criticism in recent years. Everyone would like to improve student achievement and satisfaction with school, but how should schools be restructured to accomplish these goals and better prepare our students to meet the challenges of the 21st century?

Intensive scheduling is an educational innovation that appears to be an improvement over our traditional system. The bases for intensive scheduling are the principles and strategies that many educational researchers feel are necessary for improving student achievement. What are desperately needed are more expanded studies that compare traditional scheduling against intensive scheduling.

In Conclusion

As you can see, both studies show many positive trends about intensive scheduling programs. There are three important areas that need to be considered when analyzing studies like these.

When and if you uncover a negative area of data or a troubling response to specific questions, look beyond the initial information. Ask these questions:

- Why does this happen?
- When and how does this happen?

- Is there a logical explanation?
- Is there a logical solution?

Problems may be created by other issues besides scheduling or teacher delivery. Remember the failure list at the conclusion of Chapter 1? The answer almost always lies somewhere on that list.

The schedule you select, coupled with how it is constructed and implemented, will have the greatest impact on results. The schedule is a catalyst, not a magic wand! Teachers must commit and deliver positive changes in the classroom. They must act on their training and follow through on the promises made to the key stakeholders.

Numerous studies and evaluations from across the country have me convinced that a perfect schedule does not exist. However, intensive scheduling is clearly an improvement over the other scheduling alternatives.

I truly believe that if a key change is measured consistently, it will have a great opportunity for success. I see far too many schools doing an insufficient job of measuring reform initiatives. Proper evaluation is vital in guiding the process of change and will help educators to make the right adjustments in the future.

Let's turn at last to the epilogue, which will attempt to look into the future and develop a vision for secondary schools in the 21st century.

Appendix 6-A

Intensive Scheduling - Year 6
An Evaluation of Extended Time Blocks

Hatboro-Horsham Senior High School
899 Horsham Road
Horsham, PA 19044
(215) 441-7900

Sample Daily Schedule											
8 min.		7:42 - 9:05		9:09 - 10:32		10:35 - 11:47				11:51 - 1:13		1:17 - 2:40

Period 3 columns: 3A | 3B | 3C

| Homeroom | 4 minutes | Period 1 | 4 minutes | Period 2 | 4 minutes | 3A Lunch 10:32 to 10:57 | 3B Period 3 10:57 to 11:22 | 3C 11:22 to 11:47 | 4 minutes | Period 4 | 4 minutes | Period 5 |

Whenever a new program is introduced, it is beneficial to incorporate an evaluation system in the initial planning. This provides a way to monitor the success of intensive scheduling and make adjustments to reinforce its effectiveness. One of the strengths of the Hatboro-Horsham program is that from the outset, it has a strong evaluation component built into the design of the program.

Evaluation Plan

Our evaluation plan involved the collection of 2 years of baseline data (1990-92) gathered using conventional scheduling. Identical sets of data were collected each of the first 4 years (1992-96) of intensive scheduling. Based upon empirical data, comparisons of these results gave indications of the effectiveness of the new program.

In an attempt to gather accurate and complete information, data were collected in two major categories. The quantitative data includes 12 sets of numerical facts. Qualitative information was provided from 3 sets of questionnaire responses. These data were collected each of the 6 years of the evaluation. Comparison of baseline and intensive scheduling data supplied the information to evaluate the success of the program.

Evaluation Data Categories

Quantitative Data

- Norm-Referenced Tests (NRT)
  - PSAT
    Mathematics
    Verbal
  - National Merit Scholars
  - SAT
    Mathematics
    Verbal
  - Iowa
- Teacher Grades (TG)
- Criterion-Referenced Test (CRT) / Vo-Tech Mathematics
- Attendance Summary
- Alumni Statistics
- Graduation Failure Rate
- Dropout Statistics
- PAS Test Analysis
- AP Analysis

Qualitative Data

- Questionnaire Total Responses
- Questionnaire Histograms
  Comparison of 3 Groups
  Parents
  Students
  Teachers / Administrators
- Questionnaire Written Comments

Summary of Quantitative Data (Baseline Average, BLA)

- **PSAT Analysis:** represents the following mean scores:

	BLA	1993	*1994	*1995	*1996
Math	45.2	44.7	48.1 (44.0)	49.6 (47.0)	47.7 (45.0)
Verbal	41.1	40.8	50.8 (43.0)	49.9 (42.0)	49.6 (42.0)

* In 1994, The PSAT scores were recentered. The scores in parentheses represent the equivalent results using original scores for baseline and 1993 data.

- **National Merit Scholars:**

	BLA	1993	1994	1995	1996
Semi-finalists	.5	1	0	2	3
Commended	4	2	4	6	5

- **SAT Analysis:** represents the following mean scores for college-bound seniors:

	BLA	1993	1994	1995	1996
Math	524	512	513	513	539 (520)
Verbal	458	468	453	459	547 (470)

In 1996 the SAT scores were recentered. The scores in parentheses represent scores equivalent to previous data.

• **Teacher Grades:** presented in tables below. The category "Other" includes academic exemptions, audits, withdrawals, pass/fail, and medical exemptions. (Slight discrepancies from 100% totals result from rounding.)

Marks Analysis **Examinations**

	A	B	C	D	F	I	Other
BLA	24.7%	25.3%	20.5%	15.4%	11.9%	0.6%	1.1%
Jan. 1993	19.0%	26.0%	24.0%	14.0%	8.0%	1.0%	7.0%
June 1993	18.0%	29.0%	22.0%	13.0%	9.0%	0.5%	8.5%
Jan. 1994	16.0%	26.0%	25.0%	16.0%	11.0%	1.0%	4.0%
June 1994	18.0%	28.0%	23.0%	14.0%	11.0%	1.0%	5.0%
Jan. 1995	18.0%	28.0%	25.0%	14.0%	9.0%	1.0%	6.0%
June 1995	15.0%	25.0%	29.0%	15.0%	12.0%	0.0%	4.0%
Jan. 1996	18.0%	26.0%	25.0%	13.0%	10.0%	1.0%	7.0%
June 1996	17.0%	27.0%	23.0%	15.0%	16.0%	1.0%	1.0%

Marks Analysis **Final Grades**

	A	B	C	D	F	I	Other
BLA	26.5%	33.9%	24.8%	9.5%	3.5%	0.1%	1.7%
Jan. 1993	29.0%	33.0%	21.0%	8.0%	2.0%	1.0%	7.0%
June 1993	34.0%	34.0%	20.0%	7.0%	2.0%	0.5%	2.5%
Jan. 1994	30.0%	35.0%	21.0%	9.0%	3.0%	1.0%	1.0%
June 1994	30.0%	33.0%	20.0%	8.0%	3.0%	1.0%	5.0%
Jan. 1995	30.0%	36.0%	20.0%	7.0%	4.0%	2.0%	1.0%
June 1995	30.0%	34.0%	20.0%	9.0%	4.0%	0.0%	3.0%
Jan. 1996	29.0%	35.0%	20.0%	8.0%	3.0%	2.0%	3.0%
June 1996	32.0%	34.0%	19.0%	8.0%	4.0%	1.0%	2.0%

• **Summary of Vo-Tech Mathematics (Percentage of Students Meeting Mastery Criteria):**

H-H Vo-Tech Students

	BLA	1993	1994	1995	1996
Whole Numbers	84.5%	87.9%	91.0%	81.9%	94.0%
Fractions	45.1%	50.9%	54.8%	57.6%	42.8%
Decimals	77.1%	64.7%	74.0%	62.5%	69.5%
Reading and Rounding	67.4%	74.7%	77.3%	74.1%	76.3%
Converting and Changing	48.4%	40.2%	47.3%	39.8%	45.4%
Problem Solving	70.8%	69.0%	70.0%	62.5%	61.5%
Word Problems	42.5%	34.5%	27.0%	25.0%	39.0%
Measuring and Converting	76.5%	72.4%	73.3%	79.9%	76.5%
Algebra, Geometry, Mensuration	21.0%	20.7%	23.5%	25.0%	23.5%
Scientific Notation	16.0%	24.1%	16.0%	27.8%	19.0%

• **Attendance Summary:**

			Term 1		
	BLA	1992-93	1993-94	1994-95	1995-96
Grade 9	95.2%	96.2%	95.3%	94.6%	94.8%
Grade 10	95.0%	95.3%	95.6%	93.9%	95.2%
Grade 11	95.3%	95.4%	95.4%	94.3%	95.2%
Grade 12	94.0%	95.8%	95.8%	93.2%	94.3%
Total	94.9%	95.7%	95.5%	94.1%	94.9%

			Term 2		
	BLA	1993	1994	1995	1996
Grade 9	95.3%	96.0%	93.9%	94.6%	95.3%
Grade 10	94.9%	95.2%	94.6%	94.2%	95.4%
Grade 11	95.1%	95.5%	94.3%	94.0%	94.2%
Grade 12	93.3%	95.2%	93.8%	93.0%	94.1%
Total	94.7%	95.5%	94.2%	94.0%	94.8%

• **Alumni Statistics:**

	BLA	1993	1994	1995	1996
4-Year College	45.5%	54.0%	53.0%	54.0%	55.0%
Community College	12.0%	10.0%	13.0%	11.0%	10.0%
Other 2-Year College	4.0%	4.0%	1.0%	2.0%	5.0%
Part-time College	4.0%	6.0%	10.0%	14.0%	7.0%
Vo-Tech, Nursing & Business	2.0%	2.0%	4.0%	2.0%	3.0%
Armed Forces	2.3%	4.0%	2.0%	2.0%	2.0%
Full-time Employment	5.0%	4.0%	3.0%	2.0%	7.0%
Seeking Full-time Employment	9.0%	5.0%	5.0%	3.0%	3.0%
Undecided	13.8%	11.0%	9.0%	10.0%	8.0%

• **Graduation Failure Rate:**

	BLA	1993	1994	1995	1996
(number of students who did not graduate)	17	1	7	8	3

• **Dropout Statistics:**

	BLA	1992-93	1993-94	1994-95	1995-96
(number of students who dropped out of school)	16%	12%	13%	8%	12%

• **AP Analysis**: percentages reflect students scoring 3 or better on a 5-point scale.

BLA	1992-93	1993-94	1994-95	1995-96
52%	55%	55%	57%	61%

1996 PAS Test Analysis

1996 - 9th-GRADE WRITING

MODE	SCALED SCORES	
	School	State
Narrative / Imaginative	1450	1350
Informational	1400	1340
Persuasive	1460	1380

1996 11th GRADE

READING DISTRIBUTION	School No.	%	Similar Schools %
Top 25%	82	33.2	28.8
High-Middle 25%	64	25.9	24.0
Low-Middle 25%	54	21.9	23.4
Bottom 25%	47	19.0	23.8
Totals	247	100.0	100.0

1996 11th GRADE

MATHEMATICS DISTRIBUTION	School No.	%	Similar Schools %
Top 25%	82	34.2	33.3
High-Middle 25%	65	27.1	25.1
Low-Middle 25%	66	27.5	22.0
Bottom 25%	27	11.3	19.7
Totals	240	100.0	100.0

•**Iowa Test** Scores: In **1991**, Iowa tests were administered only to students in the 9th grade. The summary is below:

% in Stanine	National	Hatboro-Horsham
7,8,9	23.0%	26.0%
4,5,6	54.0%	64.0%
1,2,3	23.0%	9.0%

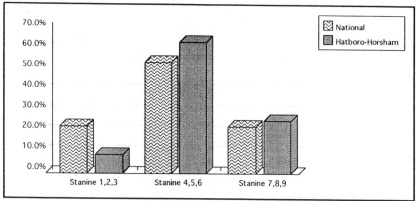

In **1992**, Iowa asked Hatboro-Horsham to participate in a series of tests to establish new norms. Therefore, there are no national norm comparisons for these data. All the students in Grades 9-12 participated. The 9th-grade summary is below:

	Reading Written Expression	Math Concepts and Problem Solving Math Computation
Average Stanine	5.5	5.6

In **1993**, only the 9th grade took the Iowa tests. The results are summarized below:

	Reading Written Expression	Math Concepts and Problem Solving Math Computation
Average Stanine	5.9	6.0

The **1994** 9th-grade Iowa results are available for comparison in both stanine and percentile forms.

	Reading Written Expression		Math Concepts and Problem Solving Math Computation	
Stanine	National	Hatboro-Horsham	National	Hatboro-Horsham
7,8,9	23.0%	45.0%	23.0%	44.6%
4,5,6	54.0%	51.8%	54.0%	50.5%
1,2,3	23.0%	3.2%	23.0%	5.0%

	Reading Written Expression	Math Concepts and Problem Solving Math Computation
Average Stanine	6.3	6.2

1995 9th-grade Iowa results compare national stanine percentages with those of Hatboro-Horsham students.

| | Reading | | Math Concepts and Problem Solving | |
| | Written Expression | | Math Computation | |
Stanine	National	Hatboro-Horsham	National	Hatboro-Horsham
7,8,9	23.0%	36.1%	23.0%	40.0%
4,5,6	54.0%	55.7%	54.0%	53.4%
1,2,3	23.0%	5.9%	23.0%	6.6%

1996 9th-grade Iowa results are graphed and summarized below.

1996 Iowa Test Score - Reading

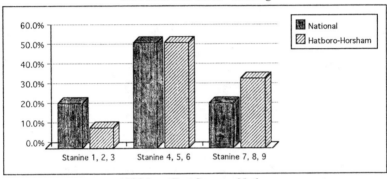

1996 Iowa Test Scores - Math

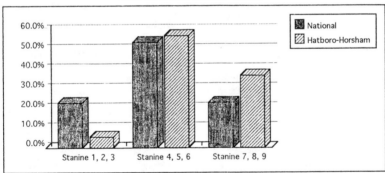

1996 9th-grade Iowa results compare national stanine percentages with those of Hatboro-Horsham students.

| | Reading | | Math Concepts and Problem Solving | |
| | Written Expression | | Math Computation | |
Stanine	National	Hatboro-Horsham	National	Hatboro-Horsham
7,8,9	23.0%	35.7%	23.0%	37.0%
4,5,6	54.0%	54.0%	54.0%	57.5%
1,2,3	23.0%	10.3%	23.0%	5.5%

Summary of **Qualitative Data** - Sample Questionnaire Responses

Twelve entries were selected from the questionnaire for inclusion in this report. The first 7 categories show the percentages of total responses in each category on the survey. The last 5 responses are represented in bar graphs to allow comparison among the responses of the 3 target groups: parents, students, and teachers/administrators.

Entry 18   A 45-minute class for 1 year is better than a 90-minute class for 1/2 year.

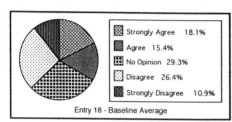

Strongly Agree	18.1%
Agree	15.4%
No Opinion	29.3%
Disagree	26.4%
Strongly Disagree	10.9%

Entry 18 - Baseline Average

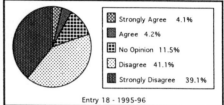

Strongly Agree	4.1%
Agree	4.2%
No Opinion	11.5%
Disagree	41.1%
Strongly Disagree	39.1%

Entry 18 - 1995-96

Entry 22   Students have many opportunities to choose electives.

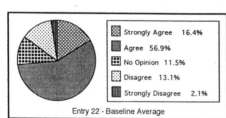

Strongly Agree	16.4%
Agree	56.9%
No Opinion	11.5%
Disagree	13.1%
Strongly Disagree	2.1%

Entry 22 - Baseline Average

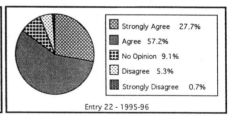

Strongly Agree	27.7%
Agree	57.2%
No Opinion	9.1%
Disagree	5.3%
Strongly Disagree	0.7%

Entry 22 - 1995-96

Entry 25   Students must be in class to keep up with classwork.

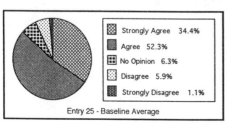

Strongly Agree	34.4%
Agree	52.3%
No Opinion	6.3%
Disagree	5.9%
Strongly Disagree	1.1%

Entry 25 - Baseline Average

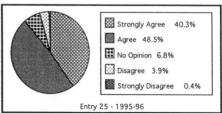

Strongly Agree	40.3%
Agree	48.5%
No Opinion	6.8%
Disagree	3.9%
Strongly Disagree	0.4%

Entry 25 - 1995-96

Entry 30   Preparing for 3 major classes for 1/2 year is better than preparing for 5
            classes for 1 year.

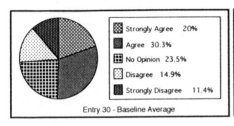

Strongly Agree	20%
Agree	30.3%
No Opinion	23.5%
Disagree	14.9%
Strongly Disagree	11.4%

Entry 30 - Baseline Average

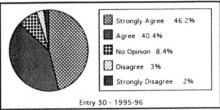

Strongly Agree	46.2%
Agree	40.4%
No Opinion	8.4%
Disagree	3%
Strongly Disagree	2%

Entry 30 - 1995-96

Entry 37   I am happy with the current scheduling in the high school.

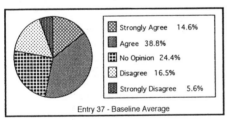

Strongly Agree	14.6%
Agree	38.8%
No Opinion	24.4%
Disagree	16.5%
Strongly Disagree	5.6%

Entry 37 - Baseline Average

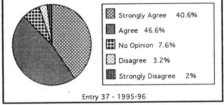

Strongly Agree	40.6%
Agree	46.6%
No Opinion	7.6%
Disagree	3.2%
Strongly Disagree	2%

Entry 37 - 1995-96

Entry 38   A 90-minute class which meets daily for 1/2 year is better for learning.

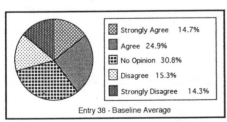

Strongly Agree	14.7%
Agree	24.9%
No Opinion	30.8%
Disagree	15.3%
Strongly Disagree	14.3%

Entry 38 - Baseline Average

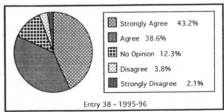

Strongly Agree	43.2%
Agree	38.6%
No Opinion	12.3%
Disagree	3.8%
Strongly Disagree	2.1%

Entry 38 - 1995-96

Entry 40   Missing class(es) for a school activity interferes with learning.

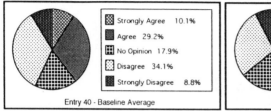

Strongly Agree   10.1%
Agree 29.2%
No Opinion 17.9%
Disagree 34.1%
Strongly Disagree   8.8%

Entry 40 - Baseline Average

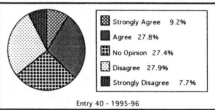

Strongly Agree   9.2%
Agree 27.8%
No Opinion 27.4%
Disagree 27.9%
Strongly Disagree   7.7%

Entry 40 - 1995-96

For the baseline years of the survey, it is not surprising that many respondents answered in the middle categories. This indicated that many were not able to assess intensive scheduling until they experienced it. Responses to more current questionnaires showed an increase in the first and last categories. Comparisons between the responses to the first 2 baseline data questionnaires (1990-92) and the last 4 intensive scheduling data questionnaires (1992-96) provided information regarding the new program which is represented graphically on the next five pages.

Entry 23   A 90-minute class for 1/2 year is better than a 45-minute class for 1 year.

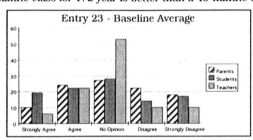

	strongly agree	agree	no opinion	disagree	strongly disagree
Parents	10%	24%	27%	22%	18%
Students	19%	22%	28%	14%	17%
Teachers	6%	22%	53%	10%	10%

Entry 23 - 1992-93

	strongly agree	agree	no opinion	disagree	strongly disagree
Parents	27.9%	41.2%	17.4%	10.5%	3.1%
Students	41.0%	37.4%	12.5%	4.4%	4.7%
Teachers	33.7%	48.2%	13.3%	2.4%	2.4%

Entry 23 - 1993-94

	strongly agree	agree	no opinion	disagree	strongly disagree
Parents	30.3%	47.4%	13.1%	5.4%	3.3%
Students	41.8%	37.4%	13.6%	4.8%	2.4%
Teachers	45.6%	38.0%	10.1%	2.5%	3.8%

Entry 23 - 1994-95

	strongly agree	agree	no opinion	disagree	strongly disagree
Parents	22.5%	64.4%	7.9%	4.5%	0.7%
Students	47.7%	36.8%	9.4%	3.4%	2.5%
Teachers	48.5%	40.4%	7.1%	1.0%	3.0%

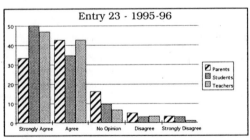

	strongly agree	agree	no opinion	disagree	strongly disagree
Parents	33.2%	42.6%	15.9%	5.1%	3.2%
Students	49.9%	34.5%	9.6%	2.9%	3.1%
Teachers	46.7%	42.4%	6.5%	3.3%	1.1%

Entry 35   A 45-minute class which meets daily for 1 year is better for learning.

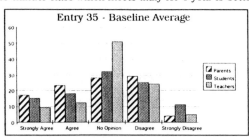

	strongly agree	agree	no opinion	disagree	strongly disagree
Parents	17%	23%	23%	29%	4%
Students	15%	18%	32%	25%	11%
Teachers	9%	12%	51%	24%	5%

Entry 35 - 1992-93

	strongly agree	agree	no opinion	disagree	strongly disagree
Parents	4.2%	12.3%	19.0%	48.8%	15.8%
Students	5.7%	5.9%	19.5%	45.0%	23.8%
Teachers	2.4%	2.4%	14.5%	60.2%	20.5%

Entry 35 - 1993-94

	strongly agree	agree	no opinion	disagree	strongly disagree
Parents	3.7%	7.0%	16.9%	52.5%	19.9%
Students	3.8%	6.7%	19.4%	42.8%	27.3%
Teachers	3.8%	0.0%	11.5%	53.8%	30.8%

Entry 35 - 1994-95

	strongly agree	agree	no opinion	disagree	strongly disagree
Parents	3.6%	7.4%	15.2%	53.8%	20.1%
Students	4.1%	6.1%	16.7%	42.4%	30.7%
Teachers	2.1%	3.1%	8.2%	56.7%	29.9%

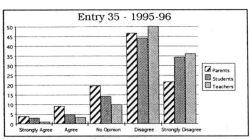

	strongly agree	agree	no opinion	disagree	strongly disagree
Parents	3.7%	8.9%	19.6%	46.5%	21.4%
Students	3.0%	4.8%	13.9%	44.0%	34.3%
Teachers	1.1%	3.3%	9.8%	50.0%	35.9%

Entry 39 Preparing for only 3 major classes for 1/2 year is better for learning.

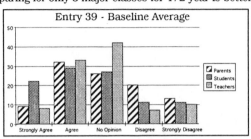

	strongly agree	agree	no opinion	disagree	strongly disagree
Parents	9%	32%	26%	20%	13%
Students	22%	29%	27%	11%	11%
Teachers	8%	33%	42%	7%	10%

Entry 39 - 1992-93

	strongly agree	agree	no opinion	disagree	strongly disagree
Parents	24.6%	49.6%	15.4%	7.7%	2.9%
Students	35.6%	45.0%	12.8%	4.0%	2.6%
Teachers	32.5%	51.8%	12.0%	1.2%	2.4%

Entry 39 - 1993-94

	strongly agree	agree	no opinion	disagree	strongly disagree
Parents	34.4%	46.1%	14.0%	3.6%	2.0%
Students	35.6%	44.6%	15.0%	3.1%	1.7%
Teachers	51.9%	38.0%	6.3%	0.0%	3.8%

Entry 39 - 1994-95

	strongly agree	agree	no opinion	disagree	strongly disagree
Parents	31.1%	51.8%	10.6%	4.7%	1.8%
Students	40.1%	45.6%	10.5%	2.5%	1.4%
Teachers	53.6%	35.1%	7.2%	3.1%	1.0%

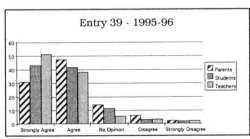

	strongly agree	agree	no opinion	disagree	strongly disagree
Parents	30.8%	47.1%	13.8%	6.2%	2.2%
Students	42.9%	41.4%	11.2%	2.8%	1.7%
Teachers	51.1%	38.0%	5.4%	3.3%	2.2%

Entry 43 I am happy to be associated with Hatboro-Horsham Senior High School.

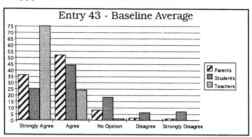

Entry 43 - Baseline Average

	strongly agree	agree	no opinion	disagree	strongly disagree
Parents	36%	52%	8%	2%	1%
Students	25%	44%	18%	6%	7%
Teachers	75%	24%	1%	0%	0%

Entry 43 - 1992-93

	strongly agree	agree	no opinion	disagree	strongly disagree
Parents	42.5%	48.8%	7.4%	.4%	.9%
Students	37.6%	41.6%	14.7%	2.8%	3.3%
Teachers	83.3%	16.7%	0.0%	0.0%	0.0%

Entry 43 - 1993-94

	strongly agree	agree	no opinion	disagree	strongly disagree
Parents	44.4%	48.4%	5.6%	0.7%	0.9%
Students	31.4%	43.9%	16.9%	4.1%	3.7%
Teachers	88.6%	11.4%	0.0%	0.0%	0.0%

Entry 43 - 1994-95

	strongly agree	agree	no opinion	disagree	strongly disagree
Parents	52.2%	40.2%	5.8%	1.6%	0.2%
Students	35.7%	44.2%	14.8%	2.6%	2.7%
Teachers	85.7%	14.3%	0.0%	0.0%	0.0%

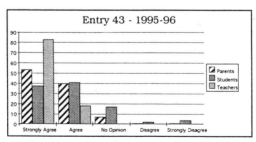

Entry 43 - 1995-96

	strongly agree	agree	no opinion	disagree	strongly disagree
Parents	52.7%	39.4%	6.5%	0.7%	0.7%
Students	37.1%	40.7%	16.9%	2.1%	3.1%
Teachers	82.6%	17.4%	0.0%	0.0%	0.0%

Entry 44 Preparing for 5 major classes for 1 year is better for learning.

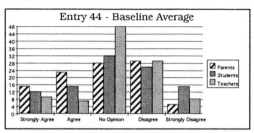

	strongly agree	agree	no opinion	disagree	strongly disagree
Parents	15%	23%	28%	29%	5%
Students	12%	15%	32%	26%	15%
Teachers	9%	7%	48%	29%	8%

Entry 44 - 1992-93

	strongly agree	agree	no opinion	disagree	strongly disagree
Parents	4.6%	11.7%	17.5%	49.8%	16.4%
Students	4.4%	6.2%	17.3%	45.0%	27.1%
Teachers	2.4%	3.6%	14.3%	59.5%	20.2%

Entry 44 - 1993-94

	strongly agree	agree	no opinion	disagree	strongly disagree
Parents	3.1%	8.3%	17.4%	48.6%	22.6%
Students	3.2%	8.3%	17.3%	44.4%	26.8%
Teachers	5.1%	0.0%	8.9%	49.4%	36.7%

Entry 44 - 1994-95

	strongly agree	agree	no opinion	disagree	strongly disagree
Parents	2.9%	8.3%	12.8%	52.8%	23.1%
Students	4.0%	7.1%	14.0%	42.8%	32.1%
Teachers	2.0%	5.1%	7.1%	50.5%	35.4%

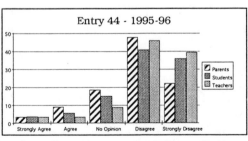

	strongly agree	agree	no opinion	disagree	strongly disagree
Parents	3.3%	8.8%	18.3%	47.6%	22.0%
Students	3.4%	5.5%	14.8%	40.6%	35.6%
Teachers	3.3%	3.3%	8.7%	45.7%	39.1%

Results of "**Teacher Only**" Questionnaire Entries

Entry 58 I am willing to try new methods of teaching in my class.

	strongly agree	agree	no opinion	disagree	strongly disagree
BLA	60.8%	33.9%	4.8%	0.5%	0.0%
1992-93	69.5%	25.6%	4.9%	0.0%	0.0%
1993-94	84.2%	15.8%	0.0%	0.0%	0.0%
1994-95	77.8%	21,1%	1.1%	0.0%	0.0%
1995-96	72.3%	25.3%	2.4%	0.0%	0.0%

Entry 59 I believe the <u>building in-service</u> program has helped me to develop strategies to teach more effectively.

	strongly agree	agree	no opinion	disagree	strongly disagree
BLA	17.2%	45.4%	18.6%	11.4%	7.4%
1992-93	22.2%	54.3%	14.8%	8.6%	0.0%
1993-94	25.0%	42.1%	17.1%	11.8%	3.9%
1994-95	22.2%	52.2%	17.8%	7.8%	0.0%
1995-96	20.5%	49.4%	16.9%	9.6%	3.6%

Entry 60 I believe the <u>district</u> staff development program has helped me to develop strategies that enable me to teach more effectively.

	strongly agree	agree	no opinion	disagree	strongly disagree
BLA	18.1%	49.1%	20.5%	6.7%	5.7%
1992-93	21.3%	55.0%	17.5%	6.3%	0.0%
1993-94	23.7%	42.5%	24.5%	9.4%	1.9%
1994-95	24.4%	46.7%	25.6%	3.3%	0.0%
1995-96	21.7%	50.6%	14.5%	10.8%	2.4%

Entry 61 I believe that a 90-minute class period will provide me with increased flexibility to use different teaching strategies.

	strongly agree	agree	no opinion	disagree	strongly disagree
BLA	25.7%	40.5%	24.2%	1.9%	7.9%
1992-93	54.3%	38.3%	3.7%	2.5%	1.2%
1993-94	67.1%	28.9%	2.6%	0.0%	1.3%
1994-95	56.4%	30.8%	8.5%	1.7%	2.6%
1995-96	69.9%	24.1%	4.8%	0.0%	1.2%

Entry 62 It is possible to effectively cover course content under the current schedule.

	strongly agree	agree	no opinion	disagree	strongly disagree
BLA	14.6%	64.4%	5.1%	13.9%	5.3%
1992-93	14.8%	51.9%	14.8%	12.3%	6.2%
1993-94	36.8%	40.8%	7.9%	10.5%	3.9%
1994-95	33.3%	51.1%	4.4%	7.8%	3.3%
1995-96	32.5%	48.2%	4.8%	7.2%	7.2%

Entry 63 Under the current schedule, it is possible to design and conduct lessons so that students use a variety of skills.

	strongly agree	agree	no opinion	disagree	strongly disagree
BLA	15.4%	69.5%	3.2%	10.4%	1.6%
1992-93	47.5%	47.5%	3.8%	6.3%	0.0%
1993-94	67.1%	31.6%	1.3%	0.0%	0.0%
1994-95	66.7%	31.1%	2.2%	0.0%	0.0%
1995-96	65.1%	31.3%	2.4%	0.0%	1.2%

Entry 64 The current scheduling allows me to achieve my professional goals.

	strongly agree	agree	no opinion	disagree	strongly disagree
BLA	16.6%	68.3%	5.4%	7.6%	2.2%
1992-93	35.8%	55.6%	4.9%	1.2%	2.5%
1993-94	59.2%	36.8%	1.3%	2.8%	0.0%
1994-95	53.8%	38.5%	4.4%	3.3%	0.0%
1995-96	51.8%	42.2%	3.6%	2.4%	0.0%

Results of "**Students Only**" Questionnaire Entries

Entry 47 As a student, I prepare for none of my tests.

	strongly agree	agree	no opinion	disagree	strongly disagree
BLA	2.9%	6.2%	10.0%	49.5%	32.1%
1992-93	1.9%	6.8%	8.4%	52.4%	30.4%
1993-94	3.6%	7.3%	12.2%	50.3%	26.6%
1994-95	2.6%	6.9%	10.8%	51.9%	27.9%
1995-96	3.7%	7.3%	11.1%	52.1%	25.8%

Entry 48 I see my teachers after school when I have questions about assignments.

	strongly agree	agree	no opinion	disagree	strongly disagree
BLA	8.9%	37.9%	17.1%	29.0%	7.3%
1992-93	5.3%	31.4%	20.6%	34.6%	8.0%
1993-94	4.7%	33.8%	25.2%	28.8%	7.5%
1994-95	11.3%	42.6%	20.3%	21.1%	4.7%
1995-96	8.5%	45.0%	18.5%	21.8%	6.2%

Entry 49 I have been scheduled for all the electives I selected.

	strongly agree	agree	no opinion	disagree	strongly disagree
BLA	27.8%	46.7%	10.0%	11.3%	5.4%
1992-93	26.7%	48.5%	8.8%	12.5%	3.4%
1993-94	24.0%	49.8%	12.0%	10.6%	3.6%
1994-95	24.0%	47.7%	12.4%	12.1%	3.7%
1995-96	25.6%	50.3%	11.5%	10.0%	2.6%

Entry 50 As a student, I prepare for some of my tests.

	strongly agree	agree	no opinion	disagree	strongly disagree
BLA	14.5%	62.0%	7.8%	12.2%	3.7%
1992-93	12.2%	63.2%	8.5%	13.5%	2.7%
1993-94	9.1%	64.0%	9.6%	13.6%	3.7%
1994-95	12.3%	62.8%	9.1%	12.3%	3.6%
1994-95	8.3%	62.0%	11.3%	13.4%	5.0%

Entry 51 As a student, I am willing to try new methods of learning.

	strongly agree	agree	no opinion	disagree	strongly disagree
BLA	26.8%	51.0%	15.0%	4.4%	3.5%
1992-93	21.6%	65.0%	9.5%	2.4%	1.6%
1993-94	20.6%	61.6%	13.6%	3.2%	1.0%
1994-95	22.4%	62.3%	11.3%	2.4%	1.7%
1995-96	20.7%	61.7%	12.5%	3.8%	1.3%

Entry 52 When I study a course for 1 year, I remember key concepts.

	strongly agree	agree	no opinion	disagree	strongly disagree
BLA	11.7%	38.4%	26.9%	17.3%	5.8%
1992-93	7.6%	31.2%	29.7%	26.2%	5.6%
1993-94	7.0%	30.6%	32.1%	24.6%	5.6%
1994-95	8.3%	24.4%	34.1%	22.9%	5.3%
1995-96	5.9%	28.4%	35.1%	24.7%	6.0%

Entry 53　As a student, I believe my responsibility is learning new ideas.

	strongly agree	agree	no opinion	disagree	strongly disagree
BLA	18.6%	56.5%	18.8%	4.9%	1.5%
1992-93	18.0%	61.9%	15.9%	3.4%	0.7%
1993-94	17.2%	57.4%	19.7%	4.5%	1.2%
1994-95	18.5%	57.3%	19.6%	3.8%	0.7%
1995-96	16.4%	57.1%	20.5%	4.4%	1.6%

Entry 54　As a student, I prepare for most of my tests.

	strongly agree	agree	no opinion	disagree	strongly disagree
BLA	17.4%	50.3%	11.1%	17.2%	4.0%
1992-93	17.1%	48.8%	11.0%	20.7%	2.5%
1993-94	15.6%	50.5%	14.3%	16.7%	3.0%
1994-95	18.2%	48.8%	13.3%	16.4%	3.3%
1995-96	15.6%	50.0%	15.1%	14.9%	4.5%

Entry 55　As a student, I understand the importance of exams.

	strongly agree	agree	no opinion	disagree	strongly disagree
BLA	23.0%	41.6%	16.2%	15.9%	3.5%
1992-93	25.0%	45.0%	13.5%	14.5%	1.8%
1993-94	22.1%	45.8%	17.1%	12.9%	2.1%
1994-95	23.4%	46.9%	16.2%	11.4%	2.2%
1995-96	22.2%	44.1%	19.3%	11.4%	2.9%

Entry 56　Under the current schedule, I remember the key concepts necessary to be successful in the next level course.

	strongly agree	agree	no opinion	disagree	strongly disagree
BLA	12.4%	41.8%	26.8%	15.5%	3.6%
1992-93	13.4%	47.6%	26.9%	8.9%	3.2%
1993-94	22.2%	45.8%	17.0%	12.9%	2.2%
1994-95	15.3%	51.2%	22.4%	9.0%	2.1%
1995-96	16.9%	51.5%	21.6%	8.4%	1.6%

Entry 57　As a student, I prepare for all of my tests.

	strongly agree	agree	no opinion	disagree	strongly disagree
BLA	16.0%	25.6%	17.7%	32.2%	8.7%
1992-93	17.9%	26.5%	17.1%	30.9%	7.6%
1993-94	15.3%	26.6%	20.0%	31.2%	6.9%
1994-95	16.3%	28.0%	20.0%	27.8%	7.9%
1995-96	15.3%	27.8%	21.9%	26.8%	8.1%

Summary of Free Response Section Comments

The tables below categorize the positive and negative comments from the free response section of the questionnaire based upon key topics identified by the respondents for the first three years of the study.

1991-93

Selected **Positive** Comments
On Intensive Scheduling

Selected **Negative** Comments
On Intensive Scheduling

Response	1991	1992	1993
Focus	30	40	263
Closure	11	19	186
Teachers	2	1	108
Grades			92
Homework			70
Electives	6	4	41
Year	3	6	39
Tests	1	2	35
Pace			17
Social	1	8	9
PE			9
College Prep	7	9	9
General			162

Response	1991	1992	1993
Teaching Style			288
Study Hall/Lunch			216
Retention	15	25	93
Attendance/Absence	1	14	87
Pace			41
Electives/Schedule			44
Homework	3	2	39
AP			34
Teachers	12	26	22
Tests	2	1	18
Year	2	2	16
Social			12
General			115

In **1993**, the first year of intensive scheduling, the number of free response comments more than doubled. In addition, comments which did not relate directly to intensive scheduling began to appear. In the summary tabulated below, the * total responses category represents all comments including those not relevant to intensive scheduling.

1993	All Groups	Students	Parents	Teachers
positive	72	41	28	3
negative	77	49	24	4
combination	682	507	134	41
* total responses	853	618	187	48

1994	All Groups	Students	Parents	Teachers
positive	57	31	22	4
negative	87	63	20	4
combination	451	326	103	22
* total responses	1468	982	416	70

1995	All Groups	Students	Parents	Teachers
positive	99	70	26	3
negative	85	58	25	2
combination	481	350	101	30
* total responses	1491	961	434	96

1996	All Groups	Students	Parents	Teachers
positive	40	14	23	3
negative	44	16	23	5
combination	194	85	84	25
* total responses	1338	1005	265	68

In an attempt to get a more accurate appraisal of the topics cited most frequently by questionnaire respondents, eight questions were attached to the free response section from 1994 through 1996. The results are summarized below. Discrepancies from 100% are the result of some questions being skipped or answered in more than one category.

	Year	**Agree**	**Disagree**
1. Intensive scheduling has enhanced the student's ability to concentrate on <u>academic work.</u>	1994	88%	10%
	1995	88%	10%
	1996	94%	6%
2. Intensive scheduling allows <u>class discussions</u> and / or <u>projects</u> to be completed more effectively.	1994	92%	7%
	1995	95%	5%
	1996	95%	5%
3. Since intensive scheduling permits students to take fewer classes each semester, they can better complete <u>homework</u> assignments and / or projects.	1994	88%	11%
	1995	90%	9%
	1996	91%	9%
4. Intensive scheduling encourages teachers to use a <u>variety of teaching styles</u> and allows time to give students <u>individual help.</u>	1994	84%	15%
	1995	88%	11%
	1996	88%	11%
5. Improvement in <u>grades</u> is directly related to intensive scheduling.	1994	69%	26%
	1995	69%	26%
	1996	67%	29%

	Year	Agree	Disagree
6. The student <u>retention</u> of course material from one level to the next has been improved by intensive scheduling.	1994	61%	30%
	1995	63%	29%
	1996	64%	29%
7. Although a variety of teaching styles are used, some teachers <u>lecture</u> for the majority of the period.	1994	63%	29%
	1995	61%	31%
	1996	61%	33%
8. <u>Study halls</u> provide sufficient time to do assigned work and/or use available <u>resource facilities</u>.	1994	80%	17%
	1995	82%	16%
	1996	80%	18%

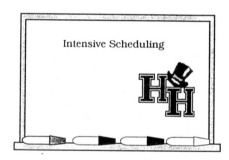

Intensive Scheduling

Special thanks for the preparation of this report are due to the members of the Evaluation Committee.

Jeanne Charlesworth	Fine and Practical Arts	Communications
John Cornelius	Administration	Quantitative
Bobbi Dorsi	Special Education	Communications
Judy Ehlenberger	Computer Education	Communications
Dorothy Graham	Mathematics (retired)	Communications
Herman Hackman	Social Studies	Qualitative
Danielle Hanna	Foreign Languages	Qualitative
Millard Hensel	Music	Qualitative
James Hessinger	School Board/Parent	Questionnaire
Margaret Kleppinger	Reading/Social Studies	Questionnaire
Dorothy Kueny	Science	Quantitative
Jennifer Labows	Graduate	Quantitative
Christopher Lake	Graduate	Qualitative
Richard Luoma	Central Administration	Quantitative
Susan Lyons	Reading/English	Questionnaire
Constance Malatesta	Administration	Proofreading
Jeanne Moon	Physical Education	Qualitative
Patricia Piano	Computer Education	Communications
Diane Stein	Library	Quantitative
James Sullivan	Administration	Communications
Ronald Tempest	Parent	Questionnaire
Ralph Wetzel	Guidance	Quantitative
James Wood	Business	Quantitative

Epilogue: A Vision for
Secondary Schools of the Future

Well-prepared, caring teachers will always hold the key to educational success. Strong leadership is also essential. The curriculum needs to be comprehensive, and technology plentiful. A variety of assessments aligned with the curriculum are needed to drive the academic program in a positive direction. The facility and resources must accommodate student and teacher needs in every way. Time and organization should be arranged meticulously to provide an efficient and effective learning environment. Even if all of these factors exist, teachers remain the most important cog in the school improvement wheel.

Higher education and K through 12 school systems across the country must collaborate to develop programs that will produce more excellent teachers in the future. The same focus and commitment are needed to produce outstanding administrative leaders as well. In my opinion, undergraduate teacher programs need to commit one full year to field experience. Either a 5-year program or a revised 4-year approach is needed. People learn to teach by being in the classroom. There is no substitute for experience. Case studies, lectures, discussion, and visual aids cannot replace real students and complex classroom scenarios.

Developing more strong school leaders is also needed if we hope to improve schools. Every national report on education points directly at leadership as essential to school success. American education needs bright, creative, and assertive leaders who will exhibit the courage needed to maintain accountability for quality results. Administrators are in demand if they do more than just manage and protect the status quo. We need school leaders who are committed to a process of change and have the ability to communicate effectively with all of the key stakeholders.

If school improvement is going to happen consistently, our governing bodies need to communicate on a regular basis with educators at all levels. Government needs to demand high expectations but keep educational policies and mandates free of politics. During the 1997 State of the Union address, President Clinton called for politics to stop at the schoolhouse door. I could not agree more! On the part of governing bodies at all levels, I see counterproductive politics hurting policy, programs, funding, and most important, children. Educators need fair and constructive accountability without question. However, educators also need support, input, and cooperation from all of the key stakeholders in America.

Parents hold a tremendous responsibility for the success of education. Parenting in America has changed as much as any issue in our society over the past 30 years. It has been well documented that there is less parenting, which has produced record numbers of dysfunctional families, than ever before in our nation's history. Typical profiles show that both parents work and spend less time with their children. Parents tend to provide for children from a material perspective but not always from an emotional standpoint. Parents want and expect schools to do more for their children because they do not have the time or motivation to act on their own. The educational platter continues to become more cluttered while parental involvement and support decline. Discipline at home is often absent, and this spillover may affect the school environment negatively. Schools are a mirror image of society. Whatever you read in the newspaper or see on TV often filters into our schools every day. These societal factors help create complex educational problems that are difficult to handle in the best of schools.

The business of improving our schools and the proficiency of our students must be shared by parents on a daily basis. Getting students to school on time, checking homework, attending meetings, and communicating with teachers are every parent's baseline responsibility. Emphasizing the importance of education and supporting school personnel is imperative. Maintaining fair but firm discipline policies at home and demanding your child's respect will have a positive impact on the school environment. All of the key stakeholders *must* do whatever it takes to develop open communication, trust, and respect. Good schools start with an orderly environment and sound discipline. I was once asked while in a school that was out of control, "What would you do first to improve this school?" I replied, "Get their attention, no matter what it takes, and then restore order." Until we have everyone's attention and a positive learning environment, schools will not improve.

Students also need to know that they have an important responsibility as part of the educational process. First, they must be actively engaged in their own education. Getting to school on time and exhibiting a positive attitude toward learning is essential. Students must try to stay healthy, and they must certainly be drug free. Students need to develop high educational and personal expectations for themselves with the help of parents and teachers. A well-thought-out priority list is needed for each child. On a consistent basis, students need to be held accountable for their behavior and performance at school. Schools must listen to students and involve them in developing policies and programs.

Students need to realize that anyone can fail. Failure does not require much intelligence or effort. Success, however, requires hard work and the courage to do one's best every day. Too many students are looking for scapegoats and excuses to justify failure. Idealistically, teachers and administrators must try to help students overcome all of the obstacles they meet. Blaming academic failures on a divorce or a fight with a friend, for example, are excuses that must be avoided at all costs. Young people of all ages need to realize that their K through 12 education is a mandatory base that every person must touch successfully if he or she hopes to live a happy and prosperous life.

In Conclusion

My travels and experiences have brought me a great deal of information on secondary school restructuring. Unfortunately, this information needs to be analyzed and organized into workable solutions. This is never an easy task, no matter what variables are present.

I am confident, however, that certain key factors and characteristics must exist in all schools if success is to be achieved. These components transcend time and will be needed for many years to come:

1. Leadership from both competent administrators and conscientious governing bodies is needed that is free from counterproductive political initiatives.

2. Adequate facilities are needed that will provide a safe and comfortable academic environment for all the curricular and cocurricular programs. Ample supplies, textbooks, and materials also need to be available for students and teachers.

3. School will be broken down into units of no more than 600 students.

4. Class size will be no more than 30 students per teacher.

5. There will be no more than 90 students per teacher per term.

6. There will be no fewer than 200 days of formal core and/or elective class time for students. Time for remedial and enrichment opportunities should also be provided.

7. Every teacher and student should be provided a laptop computer for use both inside and outside of school. This technology access should be part of a broader plan that will be well coordinated and provide for proper integration into curriculum and instruction.

8. Every teacher will have a personal plan for improvement that will include an annual technology goal tied into the individual school system's professional development objectives.

9. Every student will have a personal plan of progress that will be designed to meet the educational needs of each child.

10. A well-designed and flexible curriculum will be developed that will reflect what students really need to know (content) and be able to do (skills).

11. Accountability and measurement must be ongoing both inside the classroom and on a schoolwide basis analyzing both quantitative and qualitative data. Comprehensive evaluation will sustain the momentum of successful educational programs and guide the future course of school improvement initiatives.

12. Time must be organized flexibly and creatively to provide the most efficient and effective learning environment possible.

13. Students and parents must be committed to a quality education. These stakeholders need to openly support, communicate, and cooperate with the rest of the educational community.

14. Assessment in the classroom must be balanced between traditional and performance-based approaches. Seat time alone should not be equated with learning.

These 14 components are pillars that every school system should have in place. Unfortunately, there are no guarantees. A caring attitude, competent staff, and adequate resources will certainly provide a solid foundation for a good school. Time continues to surface as a logical starting point for the change process. Time establishes a framework that affects everything that happens at school and throughout our daily lives.

Intensive scheduling may not be the right decision for every school. It is, however, an idea that every school should consider seriously. The reconfiguration of time and organization have helped transform numerous other institutions into more successful entities. It is time for educators to follow this positive example.

Personally, I refuse to sit back and believe that our traditional approach is the best path to follow. I love to seek out problems and find creative solutions. Each year, I read the global educational test results and our own national reports with dismay. How can we so arrogantly believe that our present system is flawless and getting the job done just the way it should?

Let me focus on a well-documented national embarrassment to make my point. The United States is known worldwide for having a prison system that is second to none. Notice that I did not say the best judicial system, welfare system, health care system, or educational system, each of which is a key part of our society. In most states, we spend considerably more money to keep people in jail than we do to educate them. Something is drastically wrong with this picture! Let's work together and draw a new, improved vision that will better meet the needs of our children and society as a whole.

"Breaking ranks" from archaic traditional practices alone will not improve our system of education. After breaking away from the status quo, we must be prepared to build a stronger and more effective model. I believe that being creative with time management is the logical first step to successful secondary school restructuring. Keep an open mind, explore time change and other reform initiatives carefully, and most important, seek credible sources.

References

Cornelius, J. (1997). *An exploratory survey of intensive scheduling practices in a sample of American high schools.* Horsham, PA: Hatboro-Horsham High School.

Hatboro-Horsham High School. (1991-1996). *Six-year intensive scheduling evaluation.* Horsham, PA: Author.

National Association of Secondary School Principals. (1996). *Breaking ranks: Changing an American institution.* Reston, VA: Author.

Index

CORWIN
PRESS

The Corwin Press logo—a raven striding across an open book—represents the happy union of courage and learning. We are a professional-level publisher of books and journals for K-12 educators, and we are committed to creating and providing resources that embody these qualities. Corwin's motto is "Success for All Learners."